I0145152

# *Firsts in Sports:*
# Winning Stories

by

Paul T. Owens

Copyright © 2011 by Paul T. Owens.  All rights reserved.

Published by Myron Publishers.  No part of this publication may be reproduced, transmitted, transcribed, stored in a retrieval system, or translated into any language, in any form by any means without the written permission of the publisher; exceptions are made for brief excerpts used in published reviews.

Published by
Myron Publishers
4625 Saltillo St.
Woodland Hills, CA 91364
www.myronpublishers.com
www.paultowens.com

ISBN:978-0-9824675-1-0
Library of Congress Control Number:
Printed in the USA

This book is available for purchase in bulk by organizations and institutions at special discounts.  Please direct your inquiries to sales@MyronPublishers.com

Edited by Jo Ellen Krumm and Lee Fields.
Cover & Interior Design, Typesetting by Lyn Adelstein.

### What People Are Saying About *Firsts in Sports: Winning Stories*

"I like the way Paul included baseball with his story of football's first lawsuit."
　　—Joe DiMaggio, New York Yankees

"*Firsts in Sports: Winning Stories* is timely for today's pro-football environment, since it explains how the players and owners deal legally. The author takes you "inside" throught the eyes of the referee, with issues one can not get any other way. An interesting as well as educational read."
　　—Dr. Jim Tunney, NFL Referee 1960-91

"My good friend and great writer."
　　—Jim Murray, Los Angeles Times

Regarding the Torch Relay: "Wouldn't it be great if we could do this more often. Everyone has come together for this moment, and no one wants it to stop. We've all got a beautiful sense of being one."
　　—Bill Toomey, gold medal winner of the decathlon
　　　at the 1968 Mexico City Olympic Games

"People don't realize this, but there's more pressure on officials than there is on players."
　　—Deacon Jones, 10 time All Pro Defensive Lineman, Los Angeles Rams, talking about John McDonough, NFL referee

# About the author, Paul T. Owens

Paul T. Owens has written for the New York Times and the Los Angeles Times as a sports writer. He was coaching staff writer for the Dallas Cowboys with Tom Landry, and Senior Staff Writer with the 1984 Los Angeles Olympic Committee for Peter V. Ueberroth. He also served as Public Service Coordinator for the United States Olympic Committee.

Paul wrote biographies of National Football League officials and coaches, and for the Victor Awards, one of the longest running sports awards television shows.

He is the author of several other books, which appear on his website:

www.PaulTOwens.com.

Mr. Owens received his bachelors and masters degree in business from the University of Southern California, and attended Columbia University Writer's Program.

*Joe Di Maggio and author
Paul T. Owens,
Victor Awards
Honoring the 50th Anniversary
of Joe Di Maggio's 1941
56-game hitting streak.*

Firsts in Sports: *Winning Stories*

# Table of Contents

# Introduction

I was fortunate to have enjoyed the people I worked with as a writer for sports teams and events. From the first player in professional football who sued the NFL for his rights to the referee who ran a Super Bowl and the person who orchestrated the first Olympic Torch Relay in America, I have been involved with the excitement of great human victories and successful sport events.

The following chapters speak of firsts in sports. I am glad I was involved.

Paul T. Owens

Author Paul T. Owens with Olympic Games Administrator, Hoodie Troutman, on the 1984 Olympic Torch Relay.

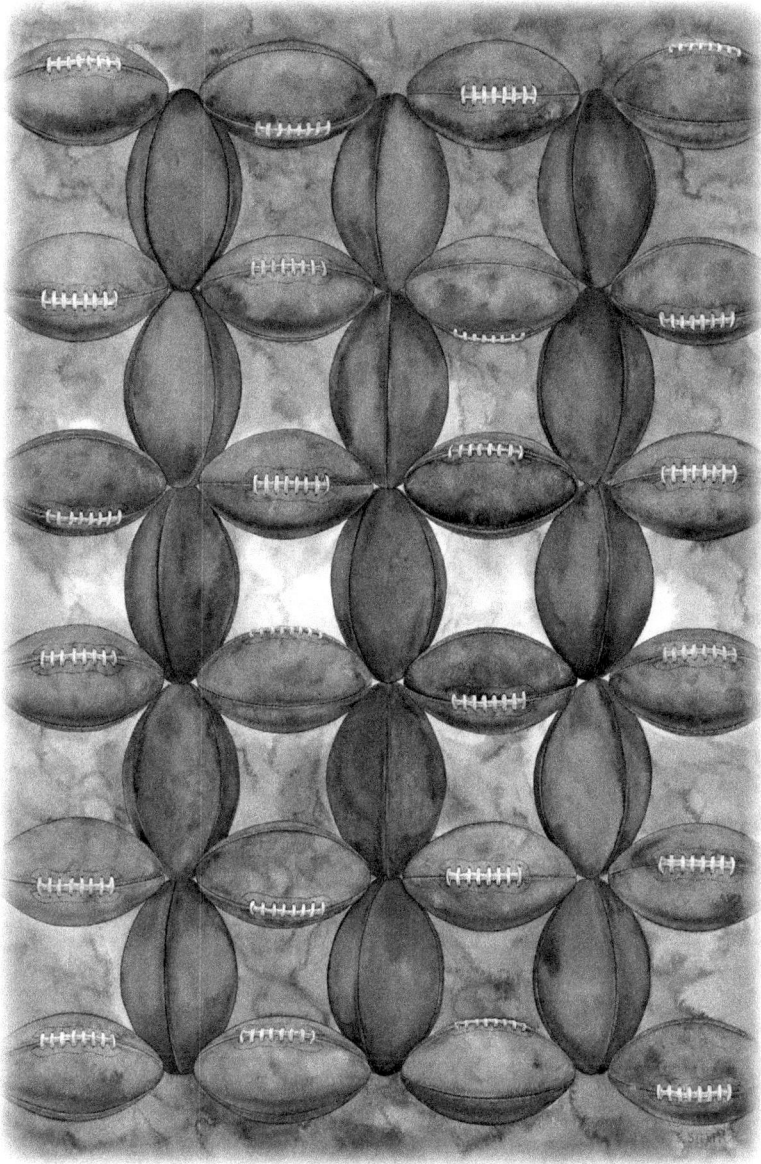

Stanley Silver, Artist

Ben Agajanian coaching the Dallas Cowboys.

# The First National Football League
# Designated Kicker Only

*Ben Agajanian was a college and professional football kicker from 1943 through 1964, the first designated kicker only player in professional football.*

*Although Ben lost the toes on his kicking foot in an elevator accident while in college, he went on to become one of the greatest kicking stars in the National Football League. He negotiated his own contract with a professional team and was the only player who ever played for no salary.*

*After he retired from kicking, he became a coach for the Dallas Cowboys for his friend, Tom Landry, and a kicking consultant for several National Football League teams.*

*He is also co- author of the book, The Kicking Game, an instructional book for kickers at all levels of football, American style. This excerpt is from his autobiography "Who's Kicking Now". Both books were co-written with Paul T. Owens.*

I do not do anything without kicking. When I was a kid, it was kicking an empty can down an alley. Then it was kicking a football in college and for fourteen professional teams, including the New York Giants and the World Champion Green Bay Packers. Now, it is teaching young kids and professional players to keep their heads down and eye on the ball while they kick. No matter where I have been, or what I am always doing, I have had one foot on the ground, and the other flying through the air. And I have been lucky. Everything that has ever happened to me off the field has made my kicking life even better.

My legs have been my best asset. The milkman proved it. He ran over both of them one day while backing out of our driveway when I was four-years-old. It was a miracle—no broken bones, a few bruises and a fifteen hundred dollar settlement. My name was not even in the program and my legs were already bringing in the money. The family used it to bring relatives to the United States from Europe.

My father was in business with my mother's brothers. Together they had interests in the rubbish and disposal industry, raising hogs, operating meat-packing houses and owning a transportation company.

As a kid I was restless and had virtually no attention span in school. I put all my energy into sports, and with my strong legs was always the best kicker. When we played kickball, I was a home run for sure. We did not call ourselves the Dodgers or the Yankees, the Lions or the Bears. We were either the Democrats or the Republicans at 15th Street School in San Pedro, California in the late '20's. Although I did not mind playing with others, I liked sports where I could compete one on one. I could not get with the team concept where you had to always hit and shove some other kid out of the way, just to show off your fourth grade "macho" skills. To me, there was nothing wrong being in the glee club either. There were not too many ways you could be hurt trying to kiss the closest soprano. And my dad always enjoyed my singing on or off key. He wanted me to be a performer.

After too many times being called too small to play on playground football teams, I decided to take up handball. I made it my business to beat everybody, and did so all through junior high school.

When I entered San Pedro High School, there was no handball team. I considered playing football but it seemed too rough for me. Besides, I could not try out for a team because I weighed one hundred and twenty-five pounds, which was too heavy for the 'C' team, and too light to be competing with one hundred and sixty pound seniors on the 'B' squad.

There was not a whole lot to see at first. I barely made the third string football team. We were so bad that even the guys sitting on the bench could not stand to watch the game. During one game the first string kicker could not get the ball off his foot. I went to the coach and offered my services. Previous experience: NONE. Well, I connected with my first one, and had to stay in the game as guard. Back then, you could not substitute unless there was a time out. I kicked a few more times before our short season ended, and spent the rest of that year on the tennis court or at the local dances.

In high school I would only dance if the girl asked me. I could not stand the rejection if I had asked someone, and she said no. It would have tarnished my winning image. But in junior college I lost my shyness and pride. I loved to jitterbug and do the New Yorker. The reality was setting in that the best girl dancers had to be asked. They were not running around, chasing after me to dance.

I made the tennis team that spring, and beat almost everybody. The following fall I went out for the football team. Head coach Tay Brown asked me what position I was going to play. I told him on the line, guard or tackle. After two plays on the line, he asked me, "What else can you do?"

"I think I can kick," I said.

"We've already got a kicker. And don't ever tell anyone you think you can. Say you can and then go out and do it."

That was high school. College at the University of New Mexico brought me more experience as a football kicker, but without the use of the toes on my kicking foot. I lost all of them in a warehouse elevator accident. I kept kicking, though, any and everywhere I could.

## WHILE THE WAR WAS ON

When my linebacker friend went to Santa Ana, California to enlist in the Air Force, he asked me to come along.

When he found they needed a kicker for the Air Base team, he recommended me. It was illegal to play for the service teams as a civilian, but I did. In my first game I set a Los Angeles Coliseum record, the first civilian to play for a service team in the stadium. A week later, November 11, 1942, I was the first person inducted into the armed services without having to take off my shoes. I was inspired to join the troops by a captain who scared me with the news, "Now that you've played for us, you have to join the armed service."

They did not need another athletic director so I enlisted as a cabinet-maker and a regular on the Santa Ana Flyers football team. Ten days later I received official notice from the Navy. They had changed their minds and were ready to accept me. The doctors had probably seen too many guys who could not walk straight. But I stayed in Santa Ana, playing out the rest of the season with the team.

The following year the team disbanded. Paul Schissler was in charge of the March Air Force football team in Riverside, California, about fifty miles from Santa Ana. He wanted me transferred to his base so I could kick for him.

Merle Hapes was with us at Santa Ana. He had joined the service after a celebrated year with the New York Giants of the NFL. When Paul asked him about me, he told him I was not worth a damn as a kicker. I put Merle up to it. Why would I want to leave Santa Ana?

The air base in Santa Ana was almost a country club. Besides, if I had left the area I would not have been able to go to San Diego on the weekends and play for the Bombers. They were paying us seventy-five dollars a game. Players from all services played. The team had players from the Marine Corps, the Air Force and the Navy. Yes, guys with three day passes were on the team. There were not too many full team practices, as the only day most of the players were all together was Sunday.

During that year I became an athletic instructor, in charge of getting cadets enthused about doing sit-ups, deep knee bends and crawling under bobbed wire fences before they were shipped overseas to battle. On Sunday, Merle Napes and I would drive down for Bombers games. It was the beginning of my career as a fly-in for the game only player.

How would you like to play with somebody else's number? Somebody else's jersey? Instead of the program saying you were six feet, three inches and weighing two hundred and forty pounds, it read that you were five feet, eight inches and weighing one hundred and seventy five pounds. For many servicemen athletes this was how it was during the Second World War. Some did not want it known that they were playing for pay. They had not received permission to play any kind of pro ball. Others were playing one weekend in San Diego, catching passes and making tackles, and the following week were being dropped onto European fields to fight real battles.

Owners of teams were not in the business of updating programs each week. "Country Austin," No. 88, had many identities under his shoulder pads, but fans only 'thought' they knew for sure who he was. They would look at the program and see his name there and say, "They must have made a mistake. It doesn't look like him but that's him, 'cause it says so right here in the program. That's his number. Last week he was 68."

NFL teams were combined during those years because so many players were in the service. In 1943 there was the Philadelphia Eagles and Pittsburgh Steelers, known as Phi-Pitt Steagles. Both teams split their home schedules, and both coaches Greasy Neale and Walt Kiesling shared their time as team leaders, working with players from both squads. The following year the Chicago Cardinals combined with the Steelers, as the Eagles had enough men to make it alone.

College teams also played service teams, and allegiances were tested. Many of the Notre Dame players who graduated in 1943 were playing for the Navy's Great Lakes Service Club in August. One of the first games on their schedule was Notre Dame.

Along with football, I played on the Santa Ana Air Base's tennis team, as its first singles player. The only player to beat me in the southern California area was Gene Mako from the Los Alamitos Naval Air Station. Losing to him was not my biggest setback. He just happened to be my partner on the national doubles championship team, even when he 'barely' beat me in matches of 6-1, 6-love.

All I cared about was that I was released on weekends, with a captain's permission, to drive to Los Angeles so I could play for the Hollywood Rangers in the newly organized American Pro Football League. No toes and all!

Our first game was against the San Francisco Clippers. We beat them 20-9, but the team lost one of its most valuable players—me. On one play I tried tackling Kenny Washington, the U.C.L.A. All-American and Clipper quarterback. I misjudged him, and my footing. My cleats planted in the grass, my legs locked, I twisted around to grab him and his elusiveness left me spinning, empty-handed. Just as I tried to regain my balance I was hit by somebody from the side. I watched the rest of the game from the bench.

The following week we played in San Diego, with my bad knee. I scored a touchdown and made two conversions. And, no, the touchdown was not made from a fumbled snap picked up for an end around kicker option. I played end, and made our quarterback look good by catching one just as it was on its way out of the end zone. The score was 31-6. Interesting to note: San Diego supported two pro teams then, the Gunners and the Bombers. They did not draw the crowds like the AFL Chargers did when they came in the '60's, but the community supported both teams at the same time during the war. The NFL has rules that try to prohibit two teams from setting up business within a seventy-mile radius. In our league there were the Los Angeles Mustangs, the Los Angeles Wolves and the Hollywood Rangers. In the other pro league on the Pacific coast during that time there were also two Los Angeles based teams—the Hollywood Wolves and the Los Angeles Bulldogs, and no one said how the competition for fan support was detrimental to the game or the league.

The inter level of play of the war years had very interesting combinations of teams playing against each other. The Cleveland Rams of 1944, later to be the Los Angeles Rams, played the Sampson Naval Base. March Air Force Base, with Paul Schissler at its football controls, played the Washington Redskins, with Dud De Groot as their coach. Coach Schissler used to tell his players, "Don't hurt the star players on the other team. We need them for the gate." It was a practice he used when he owned one of the local pro teams I played with after the war.

14

March Air Force also played the Bombers during 1944. I had been traded from Hollywood to San Diego after my injury and was on that Bomber team which lost 56-7 to Schissler. I could barely kick the ball. Some of the reverberations of the booing that the local populace graced me with, can still be heard today in San Diego. But there I was with a loser, contributing the shortest kick-off—an unintentional twelve yarder made with a knee of torn cartilage.

After the game I returned to the base in Santa Ana for a program of no strenuous exercise. The pain in my knee persisted and in January I had surgery. The operation was a success until the assistant surgeon cut the cruciate ligament. Every time I walked the knee popped in and out. I had gotten over the toes not being there to help me kick. Now I had to picture myself kicking without the help of any knee action. I could not picture it, nor could I begin thinking how I was going to change to the other foot.

Just as I began thinking of being a coach I received a call from my old coach, Coach Shipkey. He was stationed at Santa Ana and worked for the service recruiting athletes for different bases. He asked me if I wanted to go with him to a southern base to help coach a team. I think he also thought I would kick for him. Whatever his intentions and whatever thoughts I had about coaching, I did not want to be transferred out of southern California. I told him I wanted to stay home with my family. He said, fine, that he understood, but still tried to convince me how easy it would be for me if I went with him. I listened, told him how appreciative I was, but would not go.

His understanding of my position and feelings, though, did not keep him from trying to get me. In June I received a transfer notice from the top general at his base in South Carolina. And when a general asks, you go unless you have a good enough medical reason.

I went right to the officer on our base who was in charge of transfers and told him in an overdramatized case of pleading and hysterics:

"All my life, all I've wanted to do is be a coach. All my life, that's all I've wanted to do. But how would it be for me to be coaching and running a football team from a wheelchair? Look at this." I popped out my knee for him.

"But, Aggie, your orders have been requested by a general. The only way you can get out of being transferred is if you're in the hospital."

I went right to the hospital and gave the same drama about wanting to be a coach. I happened to mention that the cruciate ligament had been severed. That did it. "Hold it, Agajanian. You're not going anywhere." One doctor called the transfer officer and I told him he would write out the necessary papers that would negate the Southern General's command.

"You're going to stay with us in the hospital, too, Ben. We want to give you ten days of O and D."

"What's that?"

"That's for Observation and Disposition. We want to look at that leg. Give it some stress. See what it can and cannot do. You might be able to coach some day, but if you were planning to make a living kicking footballs, you better start looking around for something else to do."

I loved it. I was not going to the South, and the doctor apparently had not seen me the day before practicing my kicking. I did not do too well on all the tests they put me through, though, and ten days later on the Fourth of July, 1945, I was honorably discharged from the service. I was considered injured in the line of duty. Playing football in a stadium with servicemen watching was considered entertaining the troops. I was released with a pension from the Veteran's Administration. I had friends who had returned from the service without eyes and missing legs, and they received less compensation than I did for trying to tackle some errant quarterback on a twisted knee play.

What I liked about the story was that my college coach, the one who had convinced me and my family that I would play for him in college, was the guy who had unintentionally made it possible for me to be released to try out for the 1945 pro football season.

# KICKING THROUGH THE PHI-PITT STEAGLES

During my Army football days I met Jack Banta and Mel Bleeker. Both of them became members of the Philadelphia Eagles. They encouraged me to try out for the team and convinced me to write to the team's General Manager, Harry Thayer.

The team sent me a contract for two hundred dollars a game. Banta and Bleeker told me to send it back. "Ask for more."

"Why? Two hundred is good enough for me."

"Sure it is, but send it back. We always do, whether or not it's enough."

I sent it back and they sent it right back with a note attached. "Mr. Agajanian, when you make the team then you will have a chance to make more money per game."

I did not send a reply. I just boarded a plane for Philadelphia. A rookie. A nobody, and I wanted to be the best in practice. I doubled what everyone did in calisthenics. If they did twenty push-ups, I did forty. If they did ten pull-ups, I did twenty-five. I worked out with the ends, but on one day went to practice with the kickers.

The coach, Greasy Neale, came over and told me, "You're no kicker. You played end in college and did some kicking for some dingy league in California, but you're playing with the pros now. You're an end. Besides we got a kicker. Now get over there and practice your patterns."

I played in the pre-season game, and well enough I felt, to make the team. When the regular kicker was at a Sunday Army meeting, I took his place for my first pro field goal. It was also my first taste of the hatred towards kickers. On a fourth down play, instead of going for a long first down, the coach sent me in to try for a twenty-three yard three pointer. When I reached the huddle, I got a welcome reception.

"What are you doing?" one player asked.

"We don't need you. We're going for it," another said.

"I am going to kick."

"The hell you are. Now get your ass back to the bench."

I turned and ran back to the bench. The coach met me and I said, "They don't want me in there. They said they're going for it."

"You just get in there and worry about kicking the ball. Don't worry about them." He pushed me back towards the hostile group.

When I returned, one of the disgruntled players leaned back out of the huddle and announced to everybody, "It's a field goal. We're not going for it." Steven Van Buren, one of the most fabulous players during that time, grabbed the guy by the jersey and told him bluntly, "And you better block for him, too."

They all did, and I made it. But in the paper the next day another player received the credit. I could live with that. I was more concerned with the fact that the player who did not want me to try it did not even come over to say he was glad I had made it. I was out there to make the points, sure, but more than that I wanted to feel like I was appreciated by the guys I was making them for.

Even though the coach sent me in, and I made it, I did not think he liked me enough to keep me on the team. Some of the other players though got me quickly to believe otherwise. As one of them told me, "If he doesn't yell at you he doesn't like you." And, he was yelling at me, so my confidence went right up. I wired Arleen, "I got the team made. If you want to marry me wire me—YES."

She wired back, "YES—send money". I showed the telegram to a reporter and a headline read, "ROOKIE PROPOSES BY TELEGRAM." Arleen flew out from Los Angeles and we were married on September 28, 1945—the night before the first league game. The team's publicity man wanted to make it a goal post wedding—before the game or at half time—me in uniform, and Arleen dressed in a cheerleader outfit—but I said no thanks.

⇢◈⇠

I am sure some coaches would like to cut a player right in the middle of a game. After a kick wide to the left which 'lost' the game, after an unrecovered fumble, an intercepted pass which was returned for a touchdown. Yes, there have to be a few who would like to stop the game and kick the player off the team or trade him to the other side.

With the Eagles in the 1940's, the message came with intrique. The team owner's chauffeur would deliver the notice to you personally at the hotel where the players stayed. The Tuesday following the first league game, he came into the lobby where the players were waiting to go to practice. He had a few envelopes in his hand. White and edged in black. I saw him approach one of the players in the group I was in and held my breath. As he went to hand an envelope to him he looked at the name on the front of it and quickly turned and handed it to me. It was a game he played. He knew damn well who I was.

He stood there and waited for me to reach for it. When I did not, he just dropped it. It fell between my legs onto the floor. My heart went right with it. I was sick.

My ego came crashing down on top of me. I had told everyone how I was going to play ball and the first chance at it, I was told NO. My God! My dad would be right. "Football doesn't need you, and you don't need it," he had said. And now I had just been married. I was overly confident of how well I could do as a player, and I now would not have the chance.

As I stared out into the reality of cold dead space, another player said, "Don't worry about it, Aggie. Somebody'll pick you up."

"Yeah, Ben, you got a chance somewhere. Try not to take it too bad. Remember, it's just a game of big kids, a game that everybody makes too big a thing about, anyway," another player said.

"If you're not suppose to play with us, it only means you'll be with somebody else. And, probably come back to beat us one day. That's the only way to make things even."

I listened to them, but I was not ready to accept it. Playing pro ball meant too much to me. I was destroyed for a week. My wife kept things in perspective and made me believe that it was not the end of the world. I had not disappointed her, and that meant a lot to me.

Two football friends, Chuck Fenenbock and Bill Radovich, were playing with Detroit. They had told me earlier during the pre-season that if I do not make it with Philadelphia, they would see about having the Lions pick me up on waivers. I called them at the encouragement of Arleen.

Bert Bell, a part-owner of the Pittsburgh Steelers at the time, asked me if I wanted to play for Pittsburgh. I told him I was on waivers and was waiting to hear if Detroit would take me. I did not know what waivers meant at the time, but if I was on waivers, I was on waivers.

A few days later I found out I was not on waivers, and when Mr. Bell came by, I told him. He said I was free then to go with whatever team I chose. And, since no one else was standing around asking me to play for them, I went with Mr. Bell.

I found out later that I could not have been placed on waivers. The reason was the Steelers had drafted me out of college. Before the Eagles signed me, they had made an agreement with the Steelers when they were the Phi-Pitt Steagles that if I did not make the team I would belong to Pittsburgh. Mr. Bell did not volunteer the information when I was thinking about going to Detroit. I do not think he wanted to make it appear that he was forcing me to go to the Steelers.

In those days no player wanted to go to Pittsburgh. It was not just the weather. The team just lost and lost. My consideration, of course, was just to play. I did not have to play for a winner, and I was not even o the rah-rah thinking that I would or could make a team into a winner.

"All right, Mr. Bell, when do I go to Pittsburgh?"

"When can you be ready?"

"All we need is an hour to pack."

"That's good enough. I'll be back and take you to Hershey."

Arleen and I rode with Bert right to the corner of Cocoa and Chocolate Streets. The whole town smelled of sweets. It tasted good the first few days, but became boring very soon, as did everything else. The local movies changed features once a month, and the players' only release from football was more violence—the local hockey games. The players and their families lived in Hershey during the entire football season.

The 1945 Steelers gave nobody in the city anything to cheer about. We won two games and lost eight, and had the distinction of not throwing one touchdown pass the whole season. In the third game I broke my arm playing defensive end. My career was through again until they told me I could still kick for them.

"But I got a broken arm," I complained to the assistant coach.

"You're not going to kick with your arm, Agajanian. You're going to use your foot."

It turned out to be a perfect kicking season. I kicked four for four and led the league in percentage of success—1,000. I made two before the broken arm, two with it. When Bill Dudley returned to the team from the armed services, he took over some of the kicking.

I do not know if the players of that day were tougher than those playing the game now, but they sure played in more banged-up condition. Most every lineman had false teeth. The uniforms were no more protective than wearing two or three pieces of cardboard under a heavy sweater. I emerged from the season though with a blessing from that broken arm.

BECAUSE OF IT, I WAS THE FIRST PLAYER IN THE NFL TO APPEAR ON THE ROSTER AS A KICKER ONLY.

The broken arm and the loss of my toes probably made it all that more possible for me to be accepted as a kicker.

◆

During the war and the year after it the West coast had very interesting football. The competition mixtures were unusual. The team from the San Diego Naval Base played U.C.L.A. (The line average of U.C.L.A. was one hundred and ninety, backfield one hundred and seventy pounds.) The U.S.C. Trojans played the St. Mary's Preflight Airdevils. The Fleet City Blue Jackets, a service team from northern California, played the Hollywood Rangers.

U.C.L.A. All-Americans Tom Fears played for the 2nd Air Force, and Kenny Washington played for the Hollywood Bears. Elroy Hirsch—Crazylegs—of the future Los Angeles Rams was scoring for the El Toro Marines, and Bob Waterfield was the highest paid National Football League player with an annual salary for running, passing and kicking a football of twenty thousand dollars. The Rams were still in Cleveland and though they won the 1945 league title, owner Dan Reeves lost fifty thousand dollars running the ball club. And so, 1946 was the first year of the Los Angeles Rams.

The Hollywood Rangers played in the Pacific Coast League at one time. They were managed by my friend Bill Shroeder of the Citizens Savings Sports Library, and coached by Paul Schissler, who had coached in college as well as the armed services. The Signal Oil Company sponsored the club with a twenty five thousand dollar advance to begin the franchise.

Los Angeles had an abundance of local and national teams to take up fan interest in the game. More than enough. Along with the Rams and the Los Angeles Dons of the All American Football Conference, the Pacific Coast League had the Hollywood Rangers, the Los Angeles Bulldogs and the Long Beach Giants. Close by were the San Diego

Bombers. The Oakland Giants and the San Francisco Clippers were the other California teams.

In the opening game of the 1946 season we beat the Salt Lake City Seagulls 35-27 at Gilmore Stadium in Los Angeles. No field goals. I just did the extra points. For home games, attendance ranged from twenty-five hundred to six thousand. The following week we beat San Diego 28-14 at home, then we went to Salt Lake to play the Seagulls again. We lost, but the front line gained a bonus player—me. I was given the chance to play right end. I was considered big by the program roster—six feet tall, weighing two hundred pounds.

It was not until December that I had a chance to show off, though. We played the Tacoma Indians and beat them with three field goals, 9-6. One of the kicks was forty yards, another forty-seven. All of a sudden I was named the "Toeless Armenian" and the "Field Goal Artist," and I started reading my own press clippings and taking myself seriously.

One of the players on the team told me he saw one of the owners pump some helium into the ball before the game. I did not believe him. The following week, when I kicked the winning field goal to beat San Francisco 17-14, the ball barely got over the crossbar. Maybe he was right—helium was in the Tacoma game ball.

The next week we lost 10-6, but our points were scored on my kicks. One field goal was for forty-four yards, the other from forty-one yards out. After I made the first one, the thought of "helium" popped up in my mind, and I went right over to the referee and asked him if he was sure there was only air in the ball. He threw the ball up right in front of me and when he caught it, said, "What's wrong with you, Agajanian? Nothing's wrong with this ball."

During the week before the next game—the last game of the season—our coach told the press that every time we got within the forty yard line he was going to bring me in for a field goal try. I had two chances—made one and missed one. The game gave me a chance to display my talent as a multi-threat to the opposition. I scooped up an attempted lateral and ran it in for a fifty-yard score.

Because our league games were played until the end of January, some players from other pro leagues joined a few of our teams. They were not allowed to, however. The most honest play of the year in any league came when an owner of one team found a 'ringer' in his team's locker room when he came to congratulate the players on a victory. He immediately called the league's office and had the game forfeited.

Twenty-five years later I learned something else that would also have changed the standings of teams in the league. One of the owners of the Rangers was at my house for a football Sunday. When we started reminiscing about the '46 season, he told me:

"Dummy, you weren't that good. I filled the ball with half helium, half air, for one game. Their quarterback was so good I thought he'd overthrow his receivers if helium was in the ball. And he did, didn't he? It sure as hell helped you. Look how far you kicked that day. Hell, everyone thought you were a great kicker."

## LOVE A KICKER OR LOVE ME NOT

The long field goals got the attention of a few pro teams. The Los Angeles Rams and the Los Angeles Dons, along with the Washington Redskins, contacted me after my 'helium' season. The Rams and the Redskins were in the National Football League. The Dons belonged to the All America Football Conference.

The AAFC originated in 1946 to challenge the hold the NFL had on pro ball. The new conference did quite well for a while. All America Football Conference teams signed as many as one hundred NFL players, outdrew the NFL by almost ten thousand fans per game, and forced the rival existing league to pay higher player salaries.

Arch Ward, a newspaperman from Chicago, was the creator of the league. He was also director of the annual all-star game, played by the college all stars and the championship team of the NFL. Ward envisioned an expanded football country—with pro teams stretching from coast to coast. He also wanted an annual world series of football, and was aggravated that a few of his friends could not obtain NFL franchises.

With the many football players available to play after World War II, the AAFC had no trouble manning their rosters. The competition between the two leagues for players was quite stiff. The AAFC did not hold a draft their first year. The NFL in that year held its draft in secret to avoid giving the AAFC a ready-made list of players that were available for signing.

Commissioner of the AAFC, Jim Crowley, said that pro salaries increased between one hundred and two hundred percent during the competition between the two leagues and that "Should the two leagues ever agree on a common draft and hands-off policy, the figures will drop somewhat, but they will never go back to the days when a good lineman played for only $100 to $150 a game."

Rams' owner, Dan Reeves, wanted me to kick the long field goals and kickoffs. Quarterback Bob Waterfield was to do the short field goals and extra point attempts. I told Mr. Reeves, "I think I can do extra points and short field goals, just as well as Bob can," but he was just adamant about his star player doing some of the kicking. For five or six years after that meeting, I always felt a coldness with Rams management.

## KICKING ONLY

The Los Angeles Dons was a team owned mostly by Ben Lindheimer. The Dons were named after his partner, and actor, Don Ameche. The theme was Hollywood. At half time young players from the elementary schools played. Four teams played each other in the junior league— under the names of Bob Hope, Mickey Rooney, Jimmy Durante and Al Jolson. I met with Mr. Lindheimer at his home and negotiations were straight and simple. "You'll be a kicking specialist. Kicking, that's all. You don't have to do anything else."

That's what the contract said, too. "Kicking—ONLY." I did not have an attorney or agent represent me. My playing football was not that important to me that I could not do my own negotiating. I was a realist. I figured if I did not do well enough to be on the team, they would send me home anyway. No owners could accuse me of trying to milk them during contract talks. I never wanted to be in a position where I was forced to be with them; just like I did not want them to feel that I was forcing them at any time during the season to keep me on their team.

The day after I signed with the Dons I called the Redskins and told them the sad news. I am sure they got over it, soon, if not immediately, but somehow I felt that I was letting them down.

The emphasis on "Kicking only" fitted me perfectly. All the players—the other players on the Dons—had double digit numbers. I did not want two. I wanted to stand out with one. Number 3 was exact enough. I was a specialist. Exclusive to the point of not even considering myself a player.

I signed with the team in March and practiced four times a week by myself until training camp opened in August. During the second week of camp I told the coach I had to leave to take care of my business. The office was only seventy miles away from camp. I was gone only two days when my roommate called.

"Hey, you better get back up here."

"What for? The coach knows I'll be there at the end of the week in time for the Saturday scrimmage."

"You might have told him that, but there's six guys out here with kicking shoes on and they're all practicing. The coach made an announcement that you left camp and that we need a kicker."

"I'll be right up."

The next day at practice the coach came up to me and asked in front of most of the team, "Are you a businessman or football player? We're dedicated to winning football games. That's the only business you have to know while you're playing for us."

I had told the coach why I had left, and he said it was all right, but pro football was a very, very cold business. They did not give a damn. They figured maybe I was gone for good, so they needed another kicker.

In those days there were a lot of players who chose business over a pro-football career because football did not pay that well. When the coach told the team that I was gone, everybody grabbed their shoes and started kicking. They wanted to kick and maybe earn extra money for doing it. Though I was the only player hired just to kick, there were five or six players on the team who had experience kicking with NFL teams. They did not have to worry about kicking for the Dons though. I quickly had my shoes out in time to show off for the coach and get my job back as "Kicker, only."

The season opened in late August with an Intrasquad game. I kicked for both sides. Half of the team wanted me to make every kick. The other half wanted me to miss each time I tried. On my first kickoff against another team, my whole team was against me. The player making the kickoff return went right past me. I faked an effort to get him as I tried to reach the side lines. The coach saw me and grabbed me, "Why didn't you make that tackle?"

"I don't make any tackles. I am only here to kick."

"Not on this team."

"It says so in my contract. I only have to kick."

"Well, you better look like you're doing something else besides just kicking. Running away from the guy who's got the ball sure isn't the way to do it."

Mr. Lindheimer had the most specialized specialist in the league. He had ten players on the field after a kick, not eleven like the other side. How was life on the field going to be safe for me if I had to be part of the group that went down to try to bust the wedge of the kickoff return. Besides, the coaches had not signed me. The owners had.

Even the other players were aware that I was different. When I went to use the Jacuzzi, it was, "Hey, this is for the players, not the kickers." And they did not even like it when I came into the game to kick for a field goal since they could not score or make enough yardage for a first down.

I represented their frustration, even though I could help make the points. One preseason game I was called in when we were behind 16-14. They waved me off, but I came in anyway.

They held off the other team enough for me to make it and we won. But the next week, it was still their Jacuzzi, and I had to wait until all of them were through nursing themselves before I could put my foot in the door. We were billed in the game day program as America's most colorful team, but we sure did not win the award for treating each other equally.

Our division of the All America Football Conference had strong teams. There were the Cleveland Browns, San Francisco 49ers, Chicago Rockets and the Dons. In the eastern division there were the New York Yankees, Buffalo Bills, Brooklyn Dodgers and Baltimore Colts.

We broke even for the season, with a seven wins, seven losses record, but I grew in popularity by setting a league record for the most field goals in a season (15), compiling the best percentage of completions (63%), kicking the second longest field goal in professional football history (53 yards) and being the second highest scorer in the league. I also tied the field goals in one game record (3).

The things that happened were more exciting to me than the final statistics and the records. Coach Cliff Battles of the Dodgers had a "stand up" offense. The starting line got into action from an upright position instead of the traditional three-point crouch. A player who was traded away from the Dons came back on another team and kept me from trying for a record. I also got credit for winning the biggest game of the season, when the headlines should have showcased another player.

❖

We lost to Cleveland the second time we played them. Coach Dud De Groat had been replaced by Dons assistant coaches Ted Shipkey (my college coach) and the all-time center great from the New York Giants, Mel Hein. The team was accused by Paul Brown that day of dirty play, slugging, kneeing and piling on. I like what Coach Hein said in response to the charges. "We played hard, rough football all season. Brown just doesn't like our style of gang tackling the ball carrier."

No matter what Coach Brown said, he was my kind of coach. He believed in the importance of the kicking game. He gave Lou Groza the opportunity to be probably one of the greatest kickers in football. Throughout his career Lou averaged almost twice as many field goal attempts each season as other kickers in the pro leagues. Paul Brown had faith in kicking and in Groza. Although I usually give credit for my kicking success to my holder, my coaches during 1947 were most instrumental in letting me develop my kicking talent. I have always believed, and still do, that a coach makes the player; the player does not make the coach.

⬥

Glenn Dobbs, one of the best players of that era, was my holder. He held when I made a dramatic last minute field goal to beat Baltimore, 17-14. He also led both leagues with unbelievable punts in one game of seventy-two, seventy-seven, sixty, sixty-one and sixty-two yards.

For most of the 1947 and much of the 1948 seasons we outdrew the Rams. Sometimes we doubled their attendance. There was a war between the NFL and AAFC for players, and though for a while it looked like our league would survive, by the end of the 1948 season, the support was fleeting. Mr. Lindheimer had offered to help keep some of the teams alive. After the '49 season there was not much left. Only a few teams could manage financially, and they were merged with the NFL. The Cleveland Browns, Baltimore Colts and San Francisco 49ers were allowed into the other league. The players on the other clubs were distributed among the other NFL teams.

I went to the Dons' training camp in 1949. We practiced in Long Beach. The coach called me and a few other veterans in one day and told us that he was going to have to release us. The feeling with the owners, he said, was that "They want to go with youth. We're going to build for the future."

I laughed. "Well, you can build all you want for the future, but you're not going to be around to see it."

I do not know if he knew it, but there was an agreement between the two leagues at the time that the AAFC would operate for one more year before merging with the NFL. I did not take the release personally and neither did the other players who were cut. I do know he was glad to be relieved of his excessive baggage. Go ahead. Check out the 1949 roster. No player was designated as a kicker. In fact, the kicker was the guy who centered the ball to me when I was kicking. Bob Nelson did not have much of a chance, either. In a season of twelve games, he kicked only six times. It did not change my belief that one day every team would have a player who did nothing but kick. The build-for-the-future Dons lost eight times, twelve times out, on the road to extinction.

## THE KICKINGLESS GIANT

I did not have to worry about any kind of post football withdrawl after the Dons put me on their drop list.  The New York Giants called and gave me the impression that I could do a lot for them as a kicking specialist. The Mara family, owners of the team, invited me to Boystown, Nebraska to meet the team before one of their preseason games.

When I arrived there a problem of property arose. Who did I belong to? There was a question that my playing rights were still owned by the Steelers because of my 1945 affiliation with them.

I brought with me the letter that had authorized my release from Pittsburgh. It was signed by owner, Art Rooney, who had signed it in 1945 when I left the team. Wellington Mara read the letter, called Bert Bell, the current commissioner of the NFL to verify my position as being free to become a Giant. I was free to sign with them. Because I had a letter of release from Mr. Rooney I was free to play with teams in other leagues. I was not considered a "jumper," having gone to a minor league team and then playing for the other major football league.

A fellow Dons' teammate of mine, Bill Radovich, was not so fortunate. He had played with the Detroit Lions from 1938 to 1941, then joined the Navy. After the war he returned to the Lions for a season, but in 1946 asked to be traded to the Rams so he could be near his ailing father. The Lions refused. He then jumped to the All America Football Conference and played for the Dons. Since the AAFC was not affiliated with the NFL, the Dons ignored the Lions' reserve rights which at that time in sports law granted them perpetual rights to the services of every player in the league. When Radovich signed with the Dons, the NFL blacklisted him for five years. When the All America Conference folded, Bill was not hired by any pro team.

He filed a lawsuit against the NFL, charging it and its teams of conspiring to monopolize professional football in the United States by destroying the All America Football Conference and for blacklisting him. Nine years later he won a settlement against the NFL.

I was on the team, but in the worst of all positions. The owners wanted me there, but the coach was not so excited about it. There were cliques on the team. The linemen in one group, the backfield men in another. It was the days of football when athletes thought the best way to get the ball thrown to you was if you got along with the quarterback. It was a time when no one cheered for the defense; they were just the unit that was on the field while the fans waited for the offense to return from its rest along the sidelines. There was no respect for them or the kicker.

It did not help me out, either, to sleep through my first practice in Boys Town. The next day at practice Coach Owen gave me an unceremonious welcome when he announced that he was not going to have any prima donnas on the team, especially guys from California.

"Don't come after me. I'm the kicker," I shouted out to him.

Before the Philadelphia game I was talking with one of the rookies on the Eagles about how every team is out to get the other team's kicker; that some over enthused rookie wants to make the team by showing how well he can brutalize the kicker. The rookie Chuck Bednarik told me he was the one who was assigned to cover me on kickoffs. I told him I would not make any tackles if he would not try to hurt me.

"I'm not going to try to hurt you. I'm just going to knock you out of the way."

"You won't have to even touch me. I'll just casually run over to the bench after the kick."

"All right, but as soon as you hit anyone, I'm going to get two or three guys to get you."

"You got a deal." We shook hands. I felt like I just made a million dollars. It is not every day you can run into a guy who will promise he will not punch you in the mouth just for walking across a field of grass.

It worked. During the game we avoided each other, which made things unfair, eleven men were on their team, but only ten on ours for kickoffs.

With free substitution allowed, Coach Owen was able to develop his own specialists. Emlen Tunnell was used specifically on defense and led both the NFL and AAFC with ten interceptions for the season. Two rookie linemen, Al De Rogatis (defense) and Bill Austin (offense),

gave added strength to the two platoon system. Choo Choo Roberts led the league in points scored with seventeen touchdowns.

The only recognition I received was having a "K" for kicker listed next to my name on the team roster. To the coach, the "K" stood for kidding, as in, "The owners have to be kidding to have a player do nothing but kick." It certainly could have meant kidding when Charlie

Conerly, my holder, and I designed our own switch position formation in the huddle.

I was to hold the ball while Charlie kicked. The coach was not aware of it until I knelt down to catch the snap from center. When Charlie told me the signal snap was on three, I quickly blurted out, "Three! It's on three." Then I called out "one, two," and just as I was about to call out "three," the ball came back and so did the players. I barely had the ball on the ground when Charlie was there to kick it.

One of the players got Charlie good. He broke one of his ribs, and as he was being wrestled to the ground, I grabbed him, trying to keep him from going down. There was no need for any of them to tackle him. Hell, it was a try for an extra point. The other players though were mad because they thought we were rubbing it in their face by changing positions.

I got everyone out of the way and carried him back to the bench. The coach was going crazy.

"Who the hell do you think is running this damn club?"

"Let's get him a place to lie down," I said.

"Was that your idea, kicker?"

After I set Charlie down I came back to the coach. "What are you yelling at me for? We made it, didn't we?"

"And they won't forget it, either. They'll want to beat the hell out of us next time. You just wrote their pep talk for them."

The summation was simple once the season was over. I did not like living out of a hotel in New York. My daughter Lynne was born on July 14, 1949, and having a family life on the fourteenth floor was not my design of a lifestyle. Besides, I missed the business action in California where my partner had been taking care of things while I waited on the sidelines, totally out of the action. The most important consideration concerning playing football was—I was not wanted. I retired from the game and felt relieved. Football had done what I wanted it to do. My dad recognized me, and I would not have to lie to my grandchildren when they asked me, "Were you one of those guys who ran up and down the field in those crash helmets?"

## A RAM IS THIS GIANT

In March of 1953, while working at my Pine Avenue sport store in Long Beach, the Rams contacted me. One of the people in personnel asked me if I could still kick.

"Sure. I've never stopped."

"Practice up, because we would like to give you a tryout."

"When do you want me to kick for you?"

"We'll get back to you next week. Will that give you enough time?"

"That's fine."

We arranged to meet at the U.C.L.A. football practice field. When I arrived, one of the coaches came up to me and asked how far I thought I could kick.

"I can kick them in from about sixty yards out."

He laughed. "That I got to see."

"Let me warm up and I will try it for you."

I did not like his attitude so I knew I was not going to be able to wait through my usual warm-ups. I put my tee on the fifty-yard line and set the ball on top of it.

He looked at what I was doing and said, "I thought you were going to warm up."

"I am. This is where I start from."

"Don't you do any stretching?"

"I don't have to. Kicking gets me warmed up."

I stepped back and booted the ball straight through the uprights. It was one of my best kicks, everything was perfect.

"So that's your warming up, huh?" the coach asked.

"I don't know. Maybe I could do it again."

I did it again and he wanted to know, "Why don't you move it back ten and show me how you can do it from sixty yards out."

He picked up the tee and gave me a chance to make it from sixty. "Go ahead, kicker. Give me one. Even if you get it to the five yard line I'll tell the head coach you made it."

I was fuming.

I backed up and almost tripped over my feet as I set up in my beginning stance. The coach gave a slight smirk and I ran right into the ball. Short and wide to the left. He turned and signaled for some other players to come over and talk to him.

I walked over to him and grabbed him gently. "Coach, that was my warm up. I want you to see the real ones."

"I think you need a little more practice, son."

"Just stand right here and watch me."

I quickly turned and gave him two good ones from sixty yards.

"Is that enough?" I said with a smile as the other players watched for his reaction. Not bad for a kid who was playing at the young and tender age of thirty four.

"You can still kick. That's for sure. Can you come down to the office right now? We'd like to talk to you."

I signed a contract within an hour. Training camp opened on July 20, more than three months away.

On July 19, the Rams played an exhibition touch football game against the San Pedro Dolphins. It was a benefit performance to help Ram Don Simensen, a tackle whose career ended after a brain operation. Proceeds from the game went to his family to help defray medical expenses. I was half-time entertainment, booting kicks from different distances and various angles.

When the veterans checked into camp the following day, my picture was taken for the Los Angeles Times. The next day I was in the sports section with the doctor checking me over. Ten years before I had tried out for the armed services with no toes and they had told me I could not run on battlefields. Now I was being paid to kick in battle.

The Rams head coach was Hamp Pool. One of his ideas was to have me place kick out of bounds. "It would be a dangerous situation if Aggie didn't get the ball out of bounds. With him kicking, I'd send in our biggest linemen to protect him. If he missed, the safetyman could pick up the ball and make a long return before the big, slow fellows could get to him.

"But there is no reason why a kicker of Aggie's accuracy and ability shouldn't put the ball just where he wanted it. As I say, it's merely an experiment, but we're certainly going to give it a try."

With Hamp Pool, I was beginning to think I had a coach who wanted a kicker to help him. However, during practice the day before our annual intrasquad game, Night Train Lane broke through my protection too often and the coach gave up the new kicking plans. "The protection for our kickers will have to be tightened before I try that gag again," he told the press. I knew I was in for a lot of surprises when he referred to the attempted play as a 'gag.'

Our first preseason game was against the Ft. Ord Warriors. We won 72-19, scoring four of our touchdowns within a three and a half minute period. I kicked nine point after touchdowns and one field goal. On that field goal kick the ball stayed on the crossbar for a solid second before deciding to drop over on the three point side.

During the preseason we beat Cleveland 27-9, the worst beating a Browns team had taken since coming into the league in 1950. The press tried to make the game—Me vs. Lou Groza—but the rivalry never happened. I made two field goals and Lou was never given a chance to kick for three points.

I was glad we beat the Giants 21-7, but was not happy that my friend Charlie Conerly had a bad passing day for New York. I wanted to beat them but not if Charlie had to look bad.

Against the Packers, the coach reached way down in his bag of tricks when he called me into the game. I made one from forty-seven yards, but missed ones from fifty-seven and forty-two yards out. The real insult to me as a kicker was that I was sent in to make my first try when we were eighteen points ahead of Green Bay. I do not think I was considered insurance, just something to do as the last resort of offensive weaponry. I think the coach put me in to try a ridiculousy long field goal to justify having me on the team.

The newspaper said I earned my money that day from the five extra points I made along with the one field goal. I may have earned my money, but it did not go far in helping to pay for the indignity I had to face for being called into the game at no strategic points. As far as I was concerned, I was on the bottom of the roster of player appreciation.

# REDSKINS PATH TO NEW YORK

After I quit the Rams I remained on their roster until they released me to make room for Big Daddy Lipscomb. In July of 1954, I received a call from Glen Davis, a former Ram teammate. He was working for the Los Angeles Times in the capacity of coordinator of special events. The Times Charity Game that year was between the Rams and Redskins. Glen was in contact with both teams and learned that the Redskins were looking for a kicker. Curley Lambeau, the head coach of Washington, said he was interested in signing me.

When I met with the owner, George Marshall, my conditions were simple. I wanted to fly back and forth to games from Los Angeles, and be my own coach. I offered to coach the punters and back up kickers on the team, but wanted him to promise me that he would pay me an entire year's salary if they released me later than two weeks before the beginning of the regular season. I wanted to have enough time before the season began to try signing with another team.

He agreed and on July 28, I was a Redskin. "The Rams asked waivers on Aggie after he'd appeared in ten league games," was how the transaction was described in the paper the day after Washington acquired me as kicking property. I reported to training camp immediately.

My daily living schedule was the best of any player in the league. The team practiced at Occidental College, forty miles from my business. I would leave work at 4:15 and arrive just as the team was finishing its practice. I practiced kicking for an hour, went in for a rub down, had dinner with the team and then drove home at seven. I even missed the night film sessions.

The only unfortunate element was that I was resented by many of the players. By coming in the afternoon, I missed the roughest part of the Lambeau program—morning drills. He worked the team harder in the morning because he felt players were fresher then and the weather was cooler than in the afternoon. And I did not win any favor with anyone by walking onto the field while everyone else was jogging off, drenched in the dirt and sweat of the day's work. I also went to practice with a friend who was a fanatic football fan. He drove me in an over-sized Cadillac, so naturally it appeared that I was being chauffeur driven.

As a team we were considered to have a good season. At least by Mr. Marshall's standards, "I think this is the best squad we've had. It won't be our biggest squad, but it will be our best. We had so much bad luck with injuries the last two years that we feel the cycle has run its course."

Whatever were our realistic possibilities for a winning season, we had some of the winningest names in the game. Playing halfback was Charley (Choo Choo) Justice; and on the line were Slug Witucki and Moose Berschet.

I had my first chance to see how much my hamstring had healed for competitive purposes during the annual intrasquad game. I kicked for both sides and with just a little pain made a thirty-five yard field goal from a wide angle hash mark. The following week we played the Marine and Navy All Stars of the 11th district and I was able to manage seven extra points and a forty-four yard field goal in the 52-0 rout.

Our first preseason game against an NFL team was the Times Classic. We lost 27-7, but my second half kickoff was worth the price of admission. Woodley Lewis of the Rams caught the ball and ran it back ninety-five yards for a touchdown. It proved to be grounds for my first confrontation with Mr. Marshall. When I returned to the bench after the score, Mr. Marshall hollered, "Where were you on that kickoff?"

"On my ass like the rest of the guys. What do you expect out of me? I am only the kicker."

He laughed, but not for long. We lost the next week to San Francisco, 30-7. There were some misunderstandings between Curley and Mr. Marshall and Curley was fired. Joe Kuharich, an assistant, was appointed head coach. I do not think he liked kickers, and he was very open about not liking my business and late arrival schedule. He also showed a missing kick of mine over and over again during film time which did not help my morale. "Agajanian should have made that fifty yarder," he repeated. After we lost 37-7 the following week, I knew I was on my way out.

## PROTECT, CONSOLE AND LISTEN TO THE KICKER

My sensitivity was right. At the beginning of September, the staff let me know that they were going to go with another player to do the kicking. I said that was fine, according to our agreement.

They said they had traded me to the Giants and that New York wanted me to report to their training camp. I told them I was going home and that the Giants could contact me there. I was not trying to be a smart-ass or being hard to get, but I was not going to go from one team to another without the team I was going to, contacting me about the move.

I flew home from South Carolina where the Redskins were going to play next and within a few days heard from the Giants. I talked to Wellington Mara about a contract and going back and forth from my home and the games. He was not too excited about letting me be so loose with the travel arrangements.

"We are running a business here and we need you here while we're running it."

"Well my business out here needs me too, and so does my family."

"We will fly you back to New York now and discuss it when you get here. Is that fair enough?"

I knew it was usually a disadvantage to negotiate in someone else's office, but I agreed. When I met with him I was impressed with his willingness to help. He would not write it into the contract, but any time I wanted to leave for California, all I had to do was tell him.

Head Coach Jim Lee Howell had on his staff two assistants who would become two of my best football friends, and two of the most popular and successful coaches in the game, Vince Lombardi and Tom Landry. Jim Lee believed in simplicity and practice. He liked to have a team drilled well in a limited number of clear cut plays rather than hundreds of variations of specific plays. He believed football was a game of action, not a deep thinking exercise.

"We want our attack to be so simple anyone can understand it readily. We want to make the teaching of it easy, and put in our hard work on the field in practice." Lombardi felt, "When a man has to spend his time in the huddle thinking through his assignment, he often misses out."

Fortunately for me, as the kicker, there was not much I had to think about to distract me. In the beginning of the season, however, I had to get used to kicking field goals and extra points off the ground. They did not allow a kicking tee as I had been used to in college and the AAFC.

The kicking year was good for me, both on the bench and from the field. The coaches believed in kicking power, and I had the chance to help the team. I twice kicked three field goals in one game, which tied a team record, and kicked the most field goals by a Giant player with thirteen.

One of my best days was the third game of the season, against the Redskins. Charlie Conerly passed for four touchdowns, Bob Schnelker caught a record three touchdown passes and I kicked three field goals as we won 51-21. By October 21 we tied for the league lead and held it for a month. We dropped into second place on November 21, after losing to the Rams 17-16.

I made three field goals and an extra point against Los Angeles, but somehow I was blamed for losing the game. An attempted field goal kick hit the crossbar and fell down on the wrong side. No mention was made of the fact that we did not score any other way in either the third or fourth quarter. The press covered well the fact that I missed the kick. The Giants had a chance to win it, but Agajanian missed his last field goal attempt! No mention was made of how I had helped keep the team in the game. Just the negative was featured in the paper. I would not have been surprised if the press had suggested there be a search and rescue party for the kicker.

The only excuse I would have given if I had been caught is that Les Richter, the Rams defensive end, played unfairly by yelling at me before I attempted that last field goal try. If he had not, I probably would have made the kick. Blame the Giants loss on Richter, I would have told the press if they had asked why I did not make the last one.

I received some consolation from Lombardi. I had known him from the time I was with the Giants in 1949. Because I was older than the rest of the players, and not really considered a player, it was easy for me to have our friendship during the season. We spent a lot of time on trips to games, playing gin rummy and talking about his sporting goods business in New Jersey.

Vince was very protective of kickers. He did not want them to hit anyone and to 'mix it up' with the rest of the other team. Preserve the kicker was one of his unwritten rules. I had my own system of protecting myself. One way was to pay certain players to look out for me and keep other players from getting to me. The other method was to get to the bench before anyone had a chance to hit me.

I was successful with the running to the bench plan until the Giants staff used wide angle lenses to cover the entire field. The first time the team saw me on film heading for the bench they broke out laughing. Jim Lee stopped the projector and 'chewed me out.'

"You're no different from anyone, Agajanian. You go after that ball, understand?"

I just nodded my head.

When the meeting was over, Kyle Rote went over to the coach and put in a good word for me. "We get bonuses for running a certain amount of yards, if we make a tackle or an interception. Why not offer Aggie an extra bonus for kicking."

"If he wants a bonus he can go down and make tackles like everybody else does, and he may lose money if he doesn't show me he's at least trying to help in the tackling."

When Kyle told me what he said, I was excited and determined to make a tackle. The bonus for kickoff tackles was given if you tackled the man with the ball within the twenty-yard line. Two games later I pushed the kick returner out of bounds at the eighteen-yard line and was credited for a tackle inside the twenty. When I went back to the bench I was greeted by a loud chorus of cheers from the team. During that game Emlen Tunnell, the great Giant safety, encouraged me to do more. "Why don't you go down there and hit somebody else. They'll respect you for it."

## 1956 IS THE YEAR

At training camp the following year in Salem, Oregon my enthusiasm for a winning year carried on. I talked Championship with everybody, mentioning how we had recently acquired good ballplayers, and how we were going to be playing our games in Yankee Stadium. The team had acquired for the season Sam Huff, Andy Robustelli, Don Chandler, Ed Hughes, Ed Modzelewski and Gene Filipski. We were not predicted to have a great season, but we had the basic ingredients for building one. We cared about one another and had tremendous camaraderie. There were no outstanding jealousies, and as Rosey Grier, our outstanding lineman from Penn State, said, "We took care of our own problems. We did not have to go to the coaches to solve things among the players. We were a very close group."

⊰◈⊱

I flew back to New York and practiced with the team for the first home game in the new stadium. It was against Pittsburgh. Coming out onto the field before the game, we knew we would win, whomever we played. When we walked into the stadium for the game, Cliff Livingston, one of our fine defensive players, said, "How can we lose? This place is filled with such a winning history we won't be able to do anything but win. The strength of the entire place. The busts of Ruth and Gerhig just grab you and say you've got to win, too. This is a winner's house, and the strength of the history of the team stadium is passing through us, and it's going to help make us."

A lot of players heard and felt what he said. The Steelers did not have a chance. We won 38-10.

We lost only two games the rest of the season and tied the Bears, finishing with an 8-3-1 record. On December 15 we beat Philadelphia 21-7 to win the Eastern Championship. The NFL title game was scheduled for the twenty-ninth in Yankee Stadium against the Bears.

## THE CHICAGO BEARS IS OUR GAME

A few of us tried to get everyone serious about the game, but Frank Gifford kept things in a better perspective. "We haven't been serious all year, Aggie. Why should we be serious now?"

The Bears were favored, but we practiced as if it were just another game. Whatever nervousness each of us felt, we dealt with it in a light-mannered way. Practices were serious to the coaches, but somehow to the rest of us it was as if we were getting ready to march in a circus, not readying for a national athletic championship.

On the day of the game we met at Columbus Circle in Manhattan and took the subway together to Yankee Stadium. The looseness was suddenly gone. The importance of the game had taken hold in a sullen and somber mood. The pressure had squeezed each of us into a deep isolated cell, each needing to go within himself to draw out the most he could offer. All of us were concentrating on what had to be done as a team and as an individual. It was as if the love we had for each other and the total desire to win was being converted into the hate we had to have for losing.

The light-headed behavior of practice had been changed into the direct opposite, quiet, solid, steel-deep silence. Our faces looked like we had lost when we were getting ready to get aroused to come out and beat anybody. This was it.

On the train I tried talking to tackle, Dick Yelvington. He did not say anything, just sat with his head down and with tightly clenched fists. Rosey Grier, awesome with talent and personality—not saying a word. "Rosey, there is no human being on earth who can stop you if you want to get the quarterback. We're all counting on you, Rosey." Rosey nodded his head, smiled a small 'yes' at me.

I went to a few others as the train whipped, rolled and bounced underneath New York City. When we reached the dressing room the mood was so somber I wanted to scream to release the tension. Gradually the strain lessened as we started encouraging each other, Charlie Conerly had his usual pregame coughing spasms. Dick Modzelewski replaced his small contact lenses with larger ones. Jim Katcavage was his usual self, first at everything. First to get off the train and first in line to be taped by the trainer. Cliff Livingston was lying on a couch, staring at the ceiling with his playbook open and sitting on his chest.

When we got on the field we began banging each other on the shoulders to lessen the shock of initial game contact and to establish more of the physically aggressive feeling. I checked the wind's velocity and temperature. It was 22°. During the game it would dip as low as 18°. For the thin ice cover over the field we wore 'sneakers.'

We won the toss of the coin and elected to receive. Gene Filipski caught the kickoff on our nine yard line and brought it back to the Bears thirty-eight. After two unsuccessful plays, Gifford caught a floater pass from Don Heinrich and was stopped on the seventeen yard line. Mel Triplett then stormed over left tackle for the touchdown—trampling three defenders, blocking guard Jack Stroud and the umpire.

On the Bears second play from scrimmage Andy Robustelli recovered a Rick Casares fumble. Alex Webster gave us five yards, bringing the ball down to the Bears ten yard line. On the next play Triplett, being stopped cold at left end, threw the ball towards Gifford, an attempted 'pass' that fell incomplete. On third down Webster slipped at the line of scrimmage, which made it fourth and five at the ten yard line—kicking time.

As I jogged onto the field Gifford said to me, "You got your hand in my pocket, Aggie. Now put some money in it."

The kick was good and went barely over the bar. Charlie receives all the credit for having a perfect hold. As I looked up at the crossbar, he said, "What's the matter? Did you lose your power?"

"What do you expect? I got a tennis shoe on one foot. It's freezing ice and I have my cletes off my kicking shoe."

"Well, I thought you lost your power."

"How could I when I've got my holder? At least he can perform."

Following an exchange of punts between both teams, Ed Brown threw a pass which was intercepted by Giants Jim Patton, who returned the ball twenty-eight yards to the Bears thirty six yard line. After three downs of no gain—one running, two passing—I was called in for a field goal.

The wind was starting up behind me and the forty-three yard try seemed easy to make. The velocity was swift enough to take it right out of the stadium.

After the kickoff, the Bears took a risk which put them deeper in trouble. On a fourth and one situation they chose to go for a first down instead of punting. They did not make it as Emlen Tunnell and Bill Svoboda stopped J.C. Caroline short of making the necessary yard.

We took over and Gifford and Webster took turns bringing the ball down to the four yard line, where Webster took it over for the next touchdown. I converted, and the Bears were twenty points behind.

Chicago did not react well with their talent and physical force, and had to punt after their next series of downs. Emlen, however, fumbled the punt and the Bears recovered. We lost some of our momentum, and they scored five plays later with Casares going over from nine yards out.

We came back quickly. Conerly connected to Webster for a fifty yard pass play and Triplett bolted for twenty yards to the two yard line. Webster then scored, and we were twenty points ahead again. The Bears were through, but I do not think they knew it yet. After the next set of downs I think they knew for sure. Don Chandler's kickoff to them was only returned to their ten yard line. After they could not get out of their deep territory, they decided to punt from their end zone. Brown's kick was blocked and rookie Hank Moore recovered the loose ball in the end zone for six more points. Score—Giants 34, Chicago 7. I am glad we played the game at home. If we had played that well in Chicago the booing would have been unbearable.

In the third quarter, after three exchanges of the ball, we went eighty yards in three plays—one pass play from Conerly to Gifford covering sixty-nine yards. Charlie then connected to Rote all alone under the goal posts for nine yards and we led 40-7. I missed the extra point, but not on purpose—I slipped on the frozen ice field.

Early in the fourth quarter we started a march from our forty-five yard line. Gifford was nailed for a seven-yard loss, Triplett gained fifteen on a draw, and Webster powered forward for four. Conerly then passed to Gifford for twenty nine yards, and flipped the next pass to Gifford for a touchdown. Final score—Giants 47, Bears 7. Charlie was masterful all day, completing seven of ten passes for one hundred and ninety-five yards, without an interception.

The only more lopsided championship game was when the Bears beat the Redskins 73-0 in 1940. Chicago was now on the other side of a nationally-viewed spanking. I was proud being on the Giants, not only because we won when no one had predicted us to, but because the Mara family had made a tradition of owning the team throughout the years. Tim Mara, father of Wellington, bought the New York team franchise in 1925 for five hundred dollars. Thirty years later his family's team won the NFL championship, and each player on the Giants earned $3,779.00 for the day's work. Even the Bears players earned almost five times ($2,485) what it cost Tim Mara to buy a franchise.

The championship check came at a perfect time. I endorsed it over to a sports supplier to pay for some more sporting goods inventory.

"Is that what they pay you for kicking a ball in the snow?"

"Well, if the check had been for more, I'm sure you would have wanted me to pay more for the inventory." I replied.

## NEW LEAGUES COMING

My professional life was a perfect working blend—football and business. In fact I must have felt that being World Champion entitled me to go anywhere and do whatever I wanted. I wore the Giants sweat clothes everywhere, even to bed. I was the oldest kid on the block. When anyone asked who I was going to be when I grew up, I said, "I don't know. Gifford, Conerly or Sam Huff; maybe Emlen Tunnell." There I was, the oldest player on the team and telling people I was going to be a player who was ten or fifteen years younger than me.

The Giants of 1957 could not produce the glory of the year before, though we did have a winning season. Some of our players gave commercial testimonies. In a newspaper ad Dick Nolan advertised Camel cigarettes because they gave him, "richer flavor and a milder smoke." Charlie was also on billboards all over New York helping support the tobacco industry. With all that has been found negative about cigarette smoking in recent years, there is no way an NFL athlete is going to put his image in the public eye, telling everyone to score with smoking.

On September 29 we lost to the Browns in a close game determined totally by field goals. Groza had two and I had one. Two weeks later we beat the Redskins and I was fortunate to break the Washington Griffith Stadium record with a fifty-yard field goal. We had a chance to win the division until we lost to Pittsburgh 21-10.

In 1958 the Giants wanted a kicker who could double for them at an end position. They found him in Pat Summerall. Wellington called me and asked if I wanted to retire. If I chose to be retired, I would still be on their roster, and when and if another team wanted me, they would have to trade for me. I told Wellington I wanted to be released so I could be in one of my favorite positions in football—an ex-player and ready for another team to want me.

# "LET ME MAKE MY OWN TRADE."

The Western States Football League was a group of minor league teams. The franchises were to be in San Jose, Santa Ana, San Francisco, Anaheim, Costa Mesa (California) and Las Vegas. The NFL teams did not sponsor the league, but many of the general managers in the NFL were aware of the league's potential operations.

I was contacted in 1959 to be the commissioner of the conference. A meeting was held in Las Vegas among the franchise owners. I should say 'supposed' owners, because when it came time for each of them to invest their five thousand dollar initiation fee, a few of them would not. They either did not have the money or did not trust each other. At the end of the meeting, I closed up the league and called the contacts I had with the NFL teams to let them know everyone was not interested enough to make it work.

While the Western States League was disbanding, some wealthy oil men were determined to begin their own professional league. During the summer of 1959 one of the organizers of the American Football League, Lamar Hunt, aged twenty-seven, told NFL commissioner Bert Bell that he wanted the new league to merge with the existing NFL, but remain separate in the areas of scheduling and sharing profits and losses.

Mr. Bell rejected the proposal, but Hunt and Bud Adams Jr. continued their organizing efforts. Even though both leagues were concerned that competition for college players would drive salaries to the point of threatening the solvency of some franchises, the NFL would not accept a common draft. However, when AFL owners began signing NFL veteran players a few years later, the NFL owners decided to merge, or acquire the other league into its own.

My history with the AFL—my third major pro league—began when Sid Gilman, the head coach of the Los Angeles Chargers, called me from the Chargers training camp in Orange County.

"Hey, Ben. Do you think you can still kick?"

"Hell yes."

"Practice up and let me see you."

"I don't need any practice. I'm always kicking."

He started laughing. "Well, come on down then. How soon can you be here?"

"Let's see. It's Friday now. I'll be there first thing on Monday. Or do you want me to come down this afternoon?"

"No, Monday is just fine. And bring your shoes. We don't have any for a kicker who doesn't have any toes."

I showed up Monday and went out to the field. My warm-ups were a few kicks from the thirty-yard line, a couple from the forty and two perfect ones from the fifty-yard line. Bob Reifsnyder was the regular kicker. A player on the team told me that as soon as Bob saw me kick the ones from the fifty, he walked into the locker room, checked in his uniform and left camp.

After practice, Sid asked me, "Ben, my other kid, Reifsnyder left camp. (I liked that—his 'other kid' when this kid—me—was forty years old.) Did you say anything to him?"

"Say anything to him? I didn't even meet him. I saw him kicking, but I didn't talk with him."

"Well, he's gone."

"What do you have to worry about. You got an old man out of retirement to come kick for you. You should be proud of yourself for doing that."

At the end of the week he did not feel so proud. The AFI office told him that I was on another team's roster.

"Ben, you're ineligible to play for us."

"What do you mean, ineligible? Do they have an age limit?"

"No, you are not too old, but the New York Titans (later the Jets) picked you up in the dispersal draft. When we all picked players who were not with the NFL, the Titans chose you."

"They have not contacted me. Besides, they already have a kicker. They don't need me."

"Maybe they don't, but you belong back there."

"I'm not going. Why don't you let me try something."

"What do you want to do?"

"Let me call the coach and see how badly he wants me?"

I knew the coach, Sammy Baugh, but not that well. The Titans office gave me his number at the hotel where the team was staying.

The conversation between me as general manager in charge of myself went as follows:

"Coach Baugh. This is Ben Agajanian. I'm calling to congratulate you."

"Why is that, Ben?"

"I'm coming back. I'm coming out of retirement and I'm going to kick for you."

Can you imagine that. He has not seen me for years, does not know if I can kick, and there I am on his roster.

"But we're pretty well set."

"You have me on your roster, don't you?"

"We do, but..."

"I wanted to come out of retirement and kick for you."

"Well, maybe something can be done."

"I'd still like to kick. I'll tell you what I'll do, Sammy."

"What do you have in mind?"

"The Chargers have a kicker, an All-American end and kicker from Navy named Reifsnyder. He just left here today and is on his way back to New York, but he's a Charger. Why don't we make a trade; me for Reifsnyder."

"You got it."

"You go ahead and call the Chargers and tell them, and I'll go ahead and kick for Gilman."

"It's a deal. We'll get back to you."

This was unheard of in pro ball—a player making his own deal, but in the beginning of any new league things are quite spontaneous and organization is defined as it goes along.

I did not know where Bob Reifsnyder was when I talked with Coach Baugh, but he did report to the Titans and played for them during the 1960 and 1961 seasons.

# ONE COACH KNOWS HOW TO LOVE A KICKER

Sid Gilman's philosophy also included the idea, "We have a few players with no-cut contracts, but they have no more job security with the Chargers than I have. If they're not good enough to make the ball club, if they get aced out by some unsung guys, they'll be paid off and given transportation home. There is no place for the 'star system' here."

Some of the coaches, though, went on to be stars in their own right in the NFL. Assisting Sid that season were Al Davis, Chuck Noll and Jack Faulkner. The playing greats were Paul Lowe, Ron Mix and Jack Kemp, among others. The season was a success. We finished with a 10-4 record and played the Houston Oilers in the league's championship game.

During the season I had to deal with young players who were young kids when I was playing for the Dons. I was a hero to a few of them—a heroism that came back to haunt me. During the game with the Dallas Texans I came in to try for a field goal and when I reached the huddle my holder was shaking.

I asked him, "What's the matter?"

"I'm holding the ball and you're going to kick. The coach wants to see how I do under pressure."

"Well, don't worry about it. I'm the one who has the pressure."

"I know, but when I was a kid I used to go to the coliseum and watch you play."

"Some kids are up in the stands there watching you, and you better hold it well or nobody's going to remember you."

He held it all right, flat on the ground and I kicked it right into our center. We lost the game 17-0, so we could not blame the loss completely on the holder.

After the game the press descended on us. One of the newspapermen asked me, "Ben, how do you account for your poor kicking today?"

"Why, I didn't kick poorly today."

"You didn't? You missed three field goal attempts."

"No, I kicked beautifully. Every ball I hit was right on target. The wind just caught them a bit and I just missed getting them over. But I kicked perfectly."

"Oh," he said and then turned to Jack Kemp, the quarterback.

"Jack, what do you attribute your poor playing to?"

"Thanks a lot for asking me," Jack answered, then threw his helmet on the floor and walked into the shower.

Only the coach knew how to handle his athletes. When I came out of the locker room I asked Sid why he did not criticize me for not kicking well. He told me, "Ben, you're one of the best kickers I've ever seen. How could I yell at you?"

I put my arm around him and said, "Sid, you're one of the nicest guys to say that."

It was the best thing he could have done. I was his kicker and he believed in me, even when I was not doing well. His remark paid off. I made the next nine out of ten field goals. He had confidence in me and that made me want to perform well for him. My concentration even improved. The press came with praise, but no one asked me, "What do you attribute your good kicking to?"

On the way to the championship game we lost to the Boston Patriots 35-0, in a game we were favored to win. We beat Denver 23-19 in a game in which I scored three field goals and established the longest field goal kick for a Charger, the only kicker in their first regular season history—with a boot from forty-six yards out.

# PROMISE ME, PROMISE ME

The Chargers survived though and so did the league. In 1961 the team moved south to San Diego—to establish the first major pro team in that area. I met with Sid and told him, "Sid, we're good friends, but I can't go down there with you. You will need a full time kicker, one who is around all the time, and I can't move down there. I will come down and help you coach the kickers though, if you want me to."

He accepted my feelings readily and said I could have any kind of release I wanted to add to my collection of team releases. I was also selected athlete of the year by the Century Club of Long Beach for my year with the Chargers.

After I quit the Chargers it became practical joke time for some of my friends. They would call up and imitate a coach in one of the leagues and tell me they wanted me to come and kick for them. Right in the middle of the day someone would call and tell me he was Lombardi, Wellington, Gilman or Art Rooney.

One day during the beginning of the 1961 season I received a call from someone who said he was an assistant to Lamar Hunt, the owner of the Dallas Texans. "Coach Stram and Mr. Hunt would like to know if you are interested in playing in the Dallas area for the Texans."

"I'm not particularly interested, and I definitely do not want to live in Dallas."

"Well, Mr. Hunt wants you to kick for him, and so does the coach. I know Mr. Hunt will make it worth your while if you come down here and talk with us."

"Are you sure this isn't some type of joke? You know I have friends who call me all the time telling me that some team wants me to play for them, and all they're doing is kidding with me."

"Do you want me to put you on the line with Mr. Hunt?"

"No, that's all right. When do you want me to come down and talk to you?"

"As soon as possible will be soon enough for us."

"I'll fly down tomorrow, O.K.?"

I made arrangements for my flight and even though the guy sounded like the guy he said he was, I still had a feeling I was being put on. I kept asking myself during the plane trip if the whole thing was not just a hoax.

Our meeting was scheduled for two o'clock at the Holiday Inn restaurant, downtown. Two o'clock came and no assistant to Mr. Hunt. Two-fifteen and still no sign of him. At two-twenty a guy fitting the right description came into the restaurant and asked the hostess if I had arrived.

She pointed in my direction. The man came towards me, smiled and reached to shake my hand. "Lou Groza, you were always my favorite kicker."

We both laughed and sat down to discuss details about a guy who was going to fly half way across the country to kick a ball that was sitting on a field of grass. Their kicker was hurt, and they made it easy for me to say yes and make the team immediately.

I kicked in three games for the Texans. In the third game I had a vertebra dislocated on a hit while I was trying to get out of everyone's way.

A few hours after the game Coach Stram told me, "Lombardi (then coach of Green Bay) wants to trade for you. How do you feel about it?"

"Well, Hank, if you don't want me." I put it that way, but I was excited. I knew Green Bay had a definite chance to win a championship. They had lost the NFL title game the year before to the Eagles, but this year they could win it all.

"Vince has a quarterback he wants to trade for you."

"If you can't use me, I'll go then."

"It will help both of us, but I sure as hell hate to give you up."

"Whatever you want, Hank. If it will help both teams, it's fine with me."

"Don't talk about it with anyone, O.K.? We're going to keep it quiet until the deal's completed."

"Fine."

The next day the Texans equipment man snapped my back into place and I was new again.

I flew to Green Bay and began working out with the team. Bart Starr was my holder. The purpose for my being there was to take the place of Paul Hornung who was due in a few weeks to enter the armed services. During the week I received a call from Lamar.

"Aggie, will you come back and play for us one game? Paul is still in Green Bay. You can kick for us and go right back."

"Lamar, I planned on working this week with some of the players here."

"We just need you for this one game. That's all."

"Is it legal to be going back and forth between leagues like this?"

There was a pause, then Lamar said, "If you'll come back and kick this week, you can have your release right after the game and go back to play for Green Bay.'

"All right. If I can go back, I'll come."

Arleen was with me and we flew from Green Bay to Chicago's Midway Airport. From there we were taken in a helicopter to O'Hare Airport. I kept my shoes in my hand because if the luggage did not make it, at least I would be able to work the following afternoon in the Cotton Bowl, the Texans home field.

It was Arleen's birthday and what better present could I give her but a kiss from the field after setting the record for the longest field goal in the Cotton Bowl. They loved me in Dallas, but a little too much.

I flew home with Arleen, and left the next day to help open a new store in the Sunnyvale, California area near San Francisco. While I was setting up merchandise the phone rang. It was Lombardi.

"Ben, the deal is off."

"What do you mean it's off?"

"They won't release you."

"Baloney, they won't."

He laughed.

"I'll be there like I promised."

"I sure hope so, but the deal is off as far as we're concerned."

I called Hank.

"Hank, what's wrong? Vince says the deal is off."

"Aggie, how could we explain to the press and to the fans? After you came in and broke a record, everybody is crazy about you. How could we explain letting you go when we don't even have anyone right now to take your place?"

"Lamar told me that I could go back. Bill Austin was with me in Green Bay listening on the phone. Lamar spelled it out for me that I would be with the Packers after the game. I figured his word was good. I would hate to have to sue anybody, but Lamar gave me his word. If I can't play for Green Bay and for Vince, I'm not playing at all. My career is over right here."

"O.K., Aggie. If we can't talk you out of it, then good luck with the Packers."

Hank and I are still good friends, and mainly because he respected my position.

I called Vince right back. "I'm coming back."

I flew into Green Bay and finished out the season with the Packers.

## KEEPING GREEN BAY WARM

Working with Lombardi was fantastic. He was tough, fair and honest, qualities that made him both loved and respected. He had taken over a losing team, one that had a 1-10 win-loss record the year before he came and turned them into winners.

He told them right from the beginning, "I never had a losing team, and I am not going to start losing now. It's pride, loyalty, God and family that makes us win." After Vince's first season—with a 7-5 record he said the team did not win more, "because they were unaccustomed to winning."

Winning was quite important, to say the least. It was not worth it to lose. Practice after a loss was so miserable that the only way you could rebel against his strict discipline was to take it out on the next team you played. There were not too many two-game losses in a row on his coaching record.

When a player complained about his back and the work he was being put through, Vince retorted, "Your back! What about the owners' wallet and my job. It's not your back we're talking about. It's pride in what you're doing. That's what I'm talking about."

Timing was also of importance to Vince. Lombardi time meant you showed up fifteen minutes before the scheduled time. And you did not apologize if you were late. You did not have to. You were fined. He was lenient only in a few situations. I was included in one. After a practice I drove a few players to buy some extra sports shorts. While we were downtown one of us suggested we have a beer. We sat around drinking for a while and arrived at the team dinner four minutes late.

Vince met us at the cafeteria line and said we were fined fifty dollars each. We did not argue. At dinner one of the players said, "Let's tell Lombardi we just went to get the shorts."

I said, "Don't lie to Vince 'cause he knows we went and had a beer. Coaches used to be players. They know what's going on."

When we went to Vince's office, one of the players told him that it was not my fault; they had me take them downtown to buy some shorts and have a beer.

"Oh, you had a beer, huh? Well, because you're honest you're only fined thirty-five dollars. Next time don't bring me any excuses."

Vince always felt his discipline and emphasis on time is what made him successful. Everyone "off the ball" at the same time was what he practiced for every play. We would go over and over a play until every player moved at exactly the same time. When his teams were near the end zone, they were awesome. Reason: They executed their timing and coordination 'off the ball' so well that they had the jump on everybody else and performed with superiority.

Not only was Vince a great motivator, he had a keen eye for finding talent. I watched him work out a rookie once, and thought how awkward the kid was. Vince saw the talent in the player and believed he would develop. I was wrong and so were a lot of others in the team in our estimate. The player was Herb Adderly.

Vince was reasonable too. If you made a physical mistake—a fumble, an incompleted pass, poor throw, he could understand and accept it. Mental mistakes he would not stand for. The yelling and screaming from Vince was unbearable.

The only time he yelled at me was during a team meeting in New York in 1956. I did not have to attend them, but I did most of them as a sign of team spirit. On one occasion I brought a transistor radio and plugged an earphone in to listen to the World Series. While Vince was explaining a play to the team he noticed the plastic radio string hanging from my ear. He stopped and looked directly at me and was probably thinking "Aggie is getting old, and his hearing is going." A few minutes later he looked at me and smiled, as if he had figured out what I was doing, and went on with his teaching.

Ten minutes later Bill Austin, one of our guards, turned around and yelled at me, "What's the score, Aggie?"

Lombardi threw the eraser on the floor and went into a tantrum. "What are you doing?" he screamed.

"Am I bothering you?" I asked.

"Turn that damn thing off! I thought it was a hearing aid."

"Well, I'm not bothering anybody."

"What are you doing in the meeting, anyway, kicker?"

"I'm here for team spirit, coach. I could have gone to the baseball game, but I wanted to do my part in keeping the spirit up."

"Just turn it off."

Fifteen minutes later he finished explaining another play, put the chalk down, turned to me and asked, "What's the score, Aggie?"

I turned the radio back on and said, "Five to three, Yankees," and the team burst out laughing.

Vince was a genius in knowing how to be tough and when to let humor into his aggressive style. He knew how to make his team feel important, both as a unit and each man. To give them an added feel of importance he had his wife sit in the back of the team bus.

In Green Bay I gained a good friend during the season along with deepening my friendship with Vince. The new friend was Artie Funair, an assistant to Lombardi and one of the team's trainers. Artie was big in the team morale department and remembers my position of kicker as one of last resort. "Lombardi used to say, 'We got Aggie, and we'll use him if we have to, but I don't want to. I want a touchdown."

The difference between Vince saying that and most of the other coaches feeling the same was that Vince demonstrated confidence in me. He was excited about having me around for insurance. That feeling of support intensified my wanting to do well. Once again, I was wanted and appreciated.

The only thing I did not accept well during the season was a fist in my face thrown by the exuberant rookie and Hall of Fame player, Deacon Jones. Deacon had to show me he had no respect for my age or position and belted me good on one play just as I was about to make a familiar sideline exit. I would have gone after him, but we were both out of bounds on the Rams side of the field.

We beat the Rams, though, that season twice—and my other past team the Giants, once on our way to the best record for the year in the NFL. The championship game would also be the Giants and Packers. Though Green Bay had won five Western Division titles before 1961, this was the first NFL championship game ever played in Green Bay.

The game was very unexciting for Giants fans. Every quarter they went scoreless. They were held to nineteen yards rushing, had ten out of twenty-nine passes completed, with four being intercepted. Green Bay, on the other hand, gained one hundred and eighty-one yards rushing, one hundred and sixty-four yards through the air (New York receivers caught for one hundred and nineteen yards). Bart Starr completed ten of seventeen passes, without an interception!!

I was not as close with the Packers players as I was with the Giants. I wanted to have dinner with some of my old New York teammates, but it was not part of professional football protocol to have the pregame meal with members of the opposing team. Results: I ate with Gil Stratton, one of the announcers for the game.

Maybe I should have eaten with Vince. Right before the game he came up to me and said, "Ben, I want you to kick off because I don't want Paul to get hurt."

If it were another game, I would have said something to give him a bad time for what he had said, but this game was too important to start up a disagreement with him. Instead I said, "Thanks a lot, coach. All the kids are watching on television. I'll be glad to show them how to kickoff."

Vince theorized that when my 'old' legs would get cold I could not kick as far. He did not know that it was the atmospheric conditions making the differences. The ball is not going to go sixty-five yards on a kickoff in 70 below zero temperatures no matter who is kicking. His answer was to have a foot warmer on the field to keep my feet warm.

Yes, electric socks. A battery was plugged into the socks while I sat on the bench. Vince had ordered a furnace for the Green Bay bench, but Commissioner Rozelle found out about it, and made Vince get heaters for the Giants side also. So both teams were well equipped with plugged-in warmth.

After each field goal and touchdown, I would unplug the socks, run in, kickoff and run back to the bench to get replugged. After we scored our third touchdown in the second quarter, I tried to get a smile out of Vince. I went up to him and asked, "How big are the diamonds going to be on our rings?"

# THE ZERO SALARY FACTOR

The following year I returned to the Packers, as a coach for their kickers—Hornung and Jerry Kramer. When the season began I returned to Los Angeles with the understanding that I would come back if they needed me.

A few months into the season I received a call from Wayne Valley, one of the owners of the Oakland Raiders. The team had one of the worst records in the league and was on a twelve-game losing streak, having finished the season before with a 2-12 record. They needed more than a kicker. They needed to start their own league.

Mr. Valley was blunt, and so was I.

"Ben, we are desperate. We need you to play in Oakland. And, we need you now. This weekend. Could you play for us?"

"Well, I don't know."

"How much did you get with Green Bay?"

I told him approximately how much the Packers paid me.

"We can't afford to pay you that much. Would you consider playing for half that amount?"

"Wait a minute! Don't start chiseling me. Listen, I'm the chisler. That's all I do all day, but in football I never have asked for money. I'll play for nothing, but I won't have you chisel me down. If you can't pay what the Packers paid me then I'll play for nothing."

"Ben, we'd love to have you play for nothing, but I don't think that would be fair to you."

"You let me decide what is fair for me."

"All right then, when do you want to come up and join us? Can you make it before our next game? I know you like to fly in and fly out. That will be fine with us."

I flew up the day before the game and signed a contract marked zero in the area of compensation. The first contract of its kind. No percentage of the gate, or the concessions; no incentives for making so many field goals out of so many attempts. A flat salary with no longevity increments. Nothing, plain and simple.

I practiced with the center and holder so much that day my ankle went 'dead.' Why not? I was forty-two years old. On game day I kicked a lot during the pregame warm-up. Result: When I went out to kick a first field goal, my ankle could not lock and it dropped down out of place. I pushed at the ball and all it did was roll down the field. Pitiful.

It was so bad that I thought of paying the team for giving me the chance to mess up in public. However, the Raiders could not afford to fire me. Who could they get to replace me for free? I told them I would return with a better showing the following week.

Two of my children, Larry and Lynne, came with me to the next game, and we stayed in the same hotel. Sunday morning breakfast saw me with egg all over my face. I had to hide the newspaper headlines from the kids. The preview headlines for the game said, "BOOTIN' BEN KICKS LIKE MY GRANDMOTHER AND HE'S JUST AS OLD."

I made up for it almost immediately by kicking the first field goal I tried in the game. The kick was a team record field goal, but it did not help put the team on the winning track. We were too good at losing and had to keep up our consistency. The streak went to seventeen before a victory came at the last game of the season.

One of the advantages or disadvantages of playing with your team on weekends only was that all the players did not know who you were.

When I came to a Raiders meeting once, a player met me at the door and greeted me with, "You don't belong in here. This is a team meeting."

"I know. I'm Agajanian, the kicker."

"We need more than a kicker. You got a quarterback and some ends and a line with you?"

The losing spirit was widespread—both on and off the field. In the last losing game of the streak we played Houston. On one kickoff I noticed there were only nine players on the field. I yelled to the sidelines, "Hey we need two more guys out here."

Nobody came. Some of the assistants started arguing with some of the players, but no one would come so I kicked without them.

On a field goal attempt later in the game the defense broke through and blocked my kick. One of the Oilers recovered the ball and started running. I chased him but could not catch him. What made things worse was that nobody else was making much of an effort to join me. The players were more into looking at the play than being a part of it. After the Houston player made it to the end zone, I stormed over to coach Feldman. "Hey, nobody's out there with me, dammit!"

We took their kickoff but could not move the ball, so we punted. Their punt returner made a beautiful runback. On one of his cuts he came running by the sidelines. I watched intently from the bench. My frustration could not be contained. I ran onto the field and tackled him, then quickly slipped back to the bench, unnoticed by officials.

The following Tuesday the team had its first thrill of the season, watching me on film appearing in my star role. The most credit I deserved that year was for what I did in the last game of the season.

The Patriots were 9-3 coming into the game. We were 0-13 and certainly not favored, even though it was played at home and we owed our fans at least one victory to think about in the off season. Before the opening kickoff Coach Feldman said, "Kick it as deep as you can."

I said, "Why don't we try an onside kick? If they run one back when I kick it deep, there's a good chance they'll get to the forty yard line anyway."

"O.K. Go ahead and try it."

The field was perfect for it—muddy and sloppy. The ball went the required ten yards and we fell on it. The team was ecstatic. The surprise surprised the hell out of all of us. The momentum carried us to a first down, and then from the thirty-yard line I booted a three pointer. In the fourth quarter we scored a pair of touchdowns and went away beating them 17-0. We finished as winners, and were probably more excited with that one victory than players on the teams going to the championship game.

I retired again from the game—having gone out a 'winner.' Al Davis took over the Raiders the following year as head coach and winning soon became more of a tradition than a surprise which comes but once a year.

The 1962 season had a more satisfactory moment for me than the last Oakland game. In the 'other' league, the NFL, the Packers won the championship title. Green Bay beat the Giants again, 16-7. The three field goals were made from the foot of Jerry Kramer. I was glad one of my students of the field goal game had done so well.

Tommy Brooker, the kicker for Dallas that year, helped them win the AFL title, kicking two field goals as Dallas beat Houston 20-17. When I was with the Texans, I made a film for the team on kicking techniques. One of the players I worked with was Tom.

My kicking days were numbered. No one gave me desperate pleas in LA in 1963 to come back and test my ability to kick. In 1964 Sid Gilman called and said he wanted me to coach. When I went to San Diego with Arleen and started working with his kickers, Sid went over to Arleen and told her he wanted me to kick.

Arleen said, "Don't tell me, tell Aggie. He's the one who's going to do the kicking."

Sid watched me practice with the other kickers and told me, "I've seen enough. I've seen you kick and I want you to kick for us."

"I can't, Sid."

"We'll play it by ear. You don't have to sign any contract."

"I've got a commitment with Green Bay. Vince wants me to coach his kickers."

"That's all right. You can fly in from Green Bay for our games."

"All right, I'll give it a try. I'm only as good as my knees hold up. The arthritis is real bad."

Sid told the press that I was joining the Chargers again, but when the news reached Al Davis there was some doubt. Al contended that I was still a Raider and told Sid I was ineligible.

When we checked the record with AFL Commissioner Joe Foss, he found that my original contract with Oakland had the option clause crossed out. I thought I was released as a free agent after my Raider season, and could join the Chargers.

The Chargers game following the contract check was with the Raiders. While I was warming up Al came by and said, "You know you're ineligible."

"You're kidding, Al. We checked and I'm a free agent."

"No, you're not. You're ineligible to play for anyone in this league but the Raiders."

I did not say anything else to him but went over to Sid. I tapped him on the shoulder and said, "Sid, do you want me to kick? Do you want to take the chance that I could be ineligible to play for you?"

"Yeah, it's all right. Don't worry about it. Go on in there."

I went in and there was no protest after the game. Three games later, against Kansas City, it was all over anyway.

I pulled a groin muscle in practice the day before the game with the Chiefs. Because of the arthritis in my knee I did not plant my left leg solidly on the ground when I went to kick. The muscle tore and blood ran internally from the groin to the knee. To relieve the pain I was shot immediately with novocain.

They gave me five shots right before the game so I could make believe I was not hurt, but I still could not raise my leg, and my public kicking career was over. I went on the field to kick but when I realized I could not, I walked off the field.

Coach Gilman was very understanding, and I stayed with the Chargers as a coach with occasional visits to the team to help with the kickers.

The arthritis persisted in wearing away my knee and hip bones. Playing handball and working out with youngsters at my weekly coaching clinic did not help the bones' deterioration. My football afterlife still had visions of a few good kicks left in my leg. I did not receive any calls from teams for kicking services, but I was interested in helping the Dallas Cowboys when they called in preparation for the 1965 season.

## THOSE WHO CAN'T KICK, COACH

My coaching for the next few years brought me back to the Steelers, where I worked for an old friend and teammate, Bill Austin, who was then coach of Pittsburgh. I also helped George Allen in 1968 and 1969 while he was with the Rams. George Halas, one of the founders of the NFL and owner of the Chicago Bears, also invited me to look at his kickers during those two years.

When I was instructing his kickers, I stepped onto the field once and said, "Watch me this time. I want to show you how you should follow through with your kicking foot."

I booted the ball fifty yards and one of the kickers said, "Let's see you do it again." I kicked again and made it.

George was on the sidelines in his golf cart, and when I was through with my demonstration he signaled me over to him and we rode around the field for a few minutes.

"Ben, I want you to kick for us."

"I'm flattered, George, but I am almost fifty years old. I can't kick anymore."

"I just saw you make two, and it didn't look like you were fifty years old. Those kids can't make them, and they're a lot younger than you. What difference does it make how old you are? You can still kick and I want you with us."

"Today I might have done all right, but that doesn't mean I'm going to be able to kick every Sunday. I might not feel good every Sunday. I quit five years ago and I am definitely retired."

"You think about it, 'cause we want you."

I felt bad. I was wanted, but there was nothing I could do about it. The more I practiced the less effective I would be.

After practice two of the assistant coaches with the Bears took me aside.

"You're kicking for us!", one of them said.

"Oh, no. Wait a minute. I'm not kicking for anybody."

"Yes you are. Halas wants you, and you're going to kick for us."

"I know he does, but I can't."

"You can fly back and forth. You can do anything you want. All you have to do is show up and kick the ball."

"That's a great offer, but I am through as a player."

We went back and forth about who was going to kick for the team, and by the end of the night they were finally convinced that it was not going to be me.

The following day George said, "Well at least tell me about our kickers."

"They aren't too good, but your center and holder are even worse."

"What can we do about it?"

"I'd like to work with them after practice, alone. Not even with the kicker. I'll take them for forty five minutes to an hour, and they won't mind the extra time when they see their improvement."

Neither Mike Pyle, the center, nor Rich Pettibone, the holder, were excited about the arrangements. I was candid with them from the beginning.

"I've seen a lot of holders and centers, but you guys aren't worth a damn." It was not the most positive approach, but it worked.

For two weeks, every day after practice, we worked together. They perfected their timing and motion. Mac Percival, the kicker for the Bears, had a good season for Chicago that year.

The following year I went back to training camp and Pettibone and Pyle greeted me with "We'd like to show you something after practice." I stayed after and watched them center and hold. They performed the snap and hold excellently twenty-four out of twenty-five times.

That season Mac Percival was the second best kicker in the league with a sixty-nine percent (twenty-five field goals out of thirty-six attempts). The following year the Bears traded Rich Pettibone to the Rams and Percival kicked at a thirty-one percent mark (eight field goals in twenty-one attempts). Yes, the holder is evidenced somewhere in football statistics. I do not think there is any question that Pettibone had much to do with Mac's success. Pyle, of course, also contributed.

When I returned home from working with the Bears, I received a call from the Raiders. They also wanted me to look at their kickers. I flew to Oakland and the first kicker I saw was George Blanda.

"Hey, what did they hire, a kicking coach?" he quipped as I walked out onto the field.

"No, I came to take your job."

"You're not old enough."

I was almost fifty and George was forty-two at that time.

"I came to look at your other kickers," I said. "They have to have somebody ready to take your place."

"You don't have to look. I'm staying here forever. I just bought the fifty-yard line."

George holds the NFL scoring record with more than two thousand points. He played until he was forty-eight years old and had one of the best all around careers in the game—quarterbacking and kicking. He would probably still be kicking today if the Raiders had an astro turf field. Kicking for so long on grass, mud and other uneven surfaces takes its toll on your legs. But, who knows? With the advent of the smooth surface field, kickers might stay in the game until they get to their sixties. And, if they are allowed complete protection from defensive aggression, a seventy-year-old kicker is not too far out of the imagination. A lot of imagination, though.

# TOM LANDRY'S GREAT COACHES

Since 1965 I have also been a part time kicking coach for the Cowboys. Among some of the kickers I have worked with were Danny Villanueva, Mike Clark, Efren Herrera, Rafael Septien, Ron Widby, and Danny White.

The Cowboys organization has been great to me. I do most of my coaching with the kickers at the team's training camp during the summer in Thousand Oaks, California. During the season I fly to a few home games in Dallas to assist with the mid season form of their kickers.

The job keeps me young. Every summer I become a kid again. Helping a successful college kicker learn how to improve his skills is one of the greatest pleasures I have had in my life.

I explain to prospective kickers at the beginning of each training camp that I am a friend of Coach Landry and a kicking teacher. "I do not make decisions about who will be the team's kicker. I'm here only to help your kicking."

I like Tom as a coach. He chooses players who do not need rah! rah! to motivate themselves. He stresses love as a unifying team force and has an extreme gift for taking a good athlete and finding a number of positions he can play.

As a friend he has meant a lot to me. In all my life as a professional athlete he is the finest man I have known. I admire him for his beliefs and the way he treats others.

Tom picks his coaches like he does his athletes. He has some of the best people assisting him with the team. Among the great ones I have enjoyed working with are Ernie Stautner, Mike Ditka, Dan Reeves, Jim Myers, Jerry Tubbs, Gene Stallings and Ermal Allen.

"The game is played by people and judged by them, so there's bound to be mistakes."
 —Deacon Jones, 10 time All Pro Defensive Lineman, Los Angeles Rams to John McDonough

# The First American Football League Official

*"Don't Hit Him, He's Dead" is the story of the life of John*
*Mc Donough, the first official hired by the American Football*
*League in 1960 and the referee for Super Bowl IV, ten years*
*later. The book was written with Paul T. Owens. The*
*following is an excerpt from that book.*

*I wouldn't have your job for anything. When I get a tough decision,*
*I call a recess and go look it up in the book.*
        —The late Judge Franklin
            West Orange County Superior Court California.

I am tough. I have to be. For thirty-five years I was a football
official, fourteen in professional football. In stadiums filled with
a hundred thousand people I took the brunt of the booing for
those who really deserved it, the players and the coaches. That's one
reason I don't smile much. Fans never gave me standing ovations. The
people down on the field weren't rooting for me either. Players screamed
that they didn't do what I just saw them do. Coaches always wanted
me to watch the other team. Some captains wanted me to make the
penalty decisions for them. The television people thought the television
signals were more important than the signals called by the quarterback.
Owners were afraid they might lose the game, and a possible trip to the
playoffs, because we didn't see everything on every play.

That's another reason officials don't smile much. All those people
are very intense about the calls on the field and in the heat of the moment tend to interpret a smile differently. One of them might think it
was a smirk or even worse, a sneer. Such frivolity, as a smile, would indi-
cate the official wasn't taking the game very seriously, and to coaches,
owners and trainers, it is deadly serious. After all, it is their livelihood.
Occasionally, we smile anyway, but not very often.

Officials are like punching bags. Everybody's punching bag. But that's all right. We can take it. No one likes us and they don't have to. We're used to it, but just let them try playing the game without us. As referee, I was the captain of the third team on the field, the officials, sometimes called the zebras or jailbirds. I was the one who had to step out into the open all by myself and announce decisions against the home team. I was the one who coordinated television with the running of the game. I was the one responsible for keeping order in one of the world's most exciting and violent sports. There is only one referee in a game. He is the head official. He conducts the pregame officials' conference. He handles the flip of the coin. He is the one to whom the other officials report fouls. He gives the options to the captains. After they decide, he's the one who gives those funny signals.

Since the 1976 season he's been hooked up to a microphone, acting as director of fair play and administrator of retribution. The referee's position at the beginning of every scrimmage play is back there with the quarterback. From 1960 to 1974 I worked with the best quarterbacks in the country. Like many of them, I might still be there if my knees hadn't started to go, and I hadn't lost some of my speed. I still get up every Sunday wondering how I can change the TV channels so that I can get right up there and walk onto the field and start blowing the whistle again.

On October 16, 1966, Joe Namath was quarterbacking for the New York Jets. He was leading his team against the Houston Oilers and at the same time giving me advice on how I could do a better job for him. I was trying to think of how to get him to stop. First I told him that I wouldn't help him quarterback if he didn't help me referee, but that approach didn't stop him. Finally, on a third down and long yardage, Joe lofted a bomb way downfield. One of the defensive backs made a great play. He came right over the top of Joe's intended receiver, hit the ball, and knocked him to the ground. The defender had touched the ball first so there was no call for pass interference. Joe turned to me and said,

"For God's sake, why don't you go down there and call something. They're jumping all over my receivers!"

I said, "Your kicking team's coming in, Joe. See you later." Houston's offense ran three downs for a total of about five yards and kicked the ball back to the Jets. Television asked for a time out and I gave it to them. Joe and the Jets took the field and I had a whole minute before the commercial break was over.

I called, "Hey, Joe, come here."

He shuffled over. "Yeah, Big John. What do you want?"

"You see those front four?" I pointed to the Oilers line.

He nodded his head. "You got any idea how much they weigh?"

He shook his head.

"Well, I'll tell you, they've got one thing on their mind. You know what that is, Joe?"

"What's that?"

"They're gonna rip your head right off your shoulders. So, on the next four or five plays you'd better protect yourself."

"What do you mean?"

"Every time you throw the ball, Joe, I'm standing right next to you, hollering, 'Don't hit him, he's dead!' So those guys know that you've released the ball and they peel away and don't hit you. But I'm not going to be here for the next four or five plays; I'm gonna run downfield to make sure they don't mess with your receivers."

Joe looked at me, then he looked downfield. "You stay right here," he said, "The hell with the receivers."

We never had any problems for the rest of the afternoon.

In the Astrodome the entire field consisted of two pieces of astro-turf, joined in the middle by a Texas style zipper. The turf can be put down and taken up to meet the needs of any given event. Once when I came in to work a game there, I noticed the yard lines that were zipped together were slightly askew. When I told the groundskeeper, he said, "If I don't fix that, you could have a hell of an argument on your hands when they start to bring in the chains." He had it fixed, and flashed a big smile midway through the first quarter when one of the captains asked that we measure to make sure the other team had really made the first down. Now there's an important and thankless job. No public recognition in a spectacularly public place. Almost as invisible and thankless as the job of an official.

One hour before each game, an equipment manager brings 24 footballs into the officials' dressing room. The referee checks them. He is the sole judge of their legality. They must be inflated to between 12 1/2 and 13 1/2 pounds. With the advent of artificially lighted stadiums there was a problem with seeing the ball. That was solved by painting two stripes around the ball, one inch wide and about two and a half inches from each end. The pebble-grained leather has a "feel" to it which makes it easy to grip, but the painted strips were slippery. When the quarterback put his fingers on the laces and dropped his thumb over to the next panel (there are four panels on each ball) of leather, his thumb touched the painted stripe and his grip would slip. In the sixties someone had a great idea. I am not sure, but I've been told it was John Brodie, the San Francisco quarterback. He took a knife and scraped the stripe off the second panel to the left of the laces on each end of the ball. When he put the fingers of his right hand on the laces and dropped his thumb to the left he had bare leather. This eliminated the slipping. The idea was such a good one that the league had the manufacturer make all night balls with the blank panels.

Later, when lefties Ken Stabler and Bobby Douglas made their ball clubs, they put their left hand fingers on the laces and dropped their thumbs over to the right and there was that pesky stripe. So night balls were made with the stripes on the second panel to the right of the laces missing, and marked with "L" on the ball so we'd know it was for lefties. After a couple of years the striping was modified to leave a small thumb space on all four sides. With improved lighting, the visibility has ceased to be a problem and all the stripes have been removed. Now the only stripes are on our shirts.

Some quarterbacks have asked us to let them get hold of the game ball before they get it into the game. This is in line with baseball umpires who rub up the balls to take the shine off them. I told one quarterback who kept pestering me about this to write the league office. "I am not allowed to let you work with the ball until you get into the game. It's bad enough that they allow receivers to wear gloves to help them catch. Next thing you know, you guys will want to get some kind of 'completion jelly' in there and have your halfbacks use 'hand grip' so they won't fumble the ball. "I didn't mean to upset you, ref. I just wanted to get used to the ball," the quarterback said.

During rainy and snow-driven games, just try pleasing quarterbacks and centers who want dry balls all the time. Every time you wipe off the mud and the rain, it comes back as soon as the ball is put down. We tried to remedy the situation by putting a towel on the ground, but that didn't work. It got wet and players started tripping over it. Sometimes the umpire will stand with the ball and give it to the center as soon as he comes up to the line. I guess the best thing to do is offer some ideas for the all-through-the-game dry ball, or the overhead stadium cover, for the constant dry touch.

It didn't matter to me what kind of turf a game was played on. The players had to fall on it. I wasn't supposed to. Knee injuries seemed to be somewhat reduced on synthetic surfaces, but the collision type injuries, the broken shoulders and split sternums increased. When it's raining the artificial turf is great. The mud in your whistle and in your eyes and inside your pants on the natural green sure is a mess. Some of the ball clubs keep their balls from being kicked into the stands by raising a net behind the goal post. This isn't because they are cheap and don't want to lose them. They really aren't. They don't want to deny any kid having a souvenir. They just don't want anyone to get hurt.

A football at a big football game, especially the ball that was just in the game, is a tremendous 'attractive nuisance' for anyone. Especially the guy who ran clear across the stands after the touchdown to stand up there with his arms out, waiting for the ball kicked for the extra point.

The teams prevent any kind of harm to fans with the safety net. If the ball gets into the stands, some clubs will have an usher come down and retrieve it. He will get the address of the 'receiver,' and tell him that the team will send him an autographed ball during the following week. People in the stands boo when the usher comes to take the ball, but it's for everyone's safety.

"You knew, you always knew, that as serious as he acted, deep down he wanted to laugh."
—Deacon Jones, 10 time All Pro Defensive Lineman, Los Angeles Rams, speaking about John McDonough.

# New League Emerges

"Your contract is in the mail," he said.

Well, the contract came and it was for two thousand dollars for the first season. That was a lot more than I had ever received working in the college ranks. Bob told me later that because I was the first official in the league to sign and return a contract, he gave me the lowest number, #11, which I kept until I retired.

My friends told me I was crazy. The National Football League would bury these people in the new league. "No way it's going to make it," they said of the American Football League (AFL).

I told them that I was betting it would be different. That was 1959.

They had good reason to think that way. There had been other leagues in the history of pro football to challenge the existing National Football League that did not last. Three of them were called the American Football League, coincidentally (1920, 1936, 1940). One of them was called the All-America Football Conference (1946). The teams in those leagues either became part of the National Football League or disbanded due to lack of serious fan support.

Things started to jell for the AFL this time. We had our first officials' clinic, in Dallas, Texas, and I was appointed as a referee of a five-man crew. On our crew was Clyde Devine, the umpire, who was my supervising teacher when I was a student teacher at Sequoia High School in Redwood City, California. Clyde had worked in the old All America Conference and then in the National Football League and here he was with us in the beginning of the American Football League. Elvin Hutchison was the head lincsman. He, too, had been in the National Football League. He and Gil Castree had told Bob Austin they would come over to the new league and help him break in the new pro officials. We were very fortunate to have Elvin and his experience on our crew.

Our line judge was Willard "Lefty" Goodhue, one of the top officials in Southern California. Our field judge was Chuck Liley, a highly regarded college official from Denver, Colorado. There were only five men on a crew then. In 1962 the AFL followed the lead of the NFL and added a sixth man, the back judge, and in 1978, the seventh man, the side judge, was added.

The AFL games were more wide open than the NFL. Scores were higher. There were only three-man front lines on defense, and zone defenses were used. The moving pocket was an innovation of the AFL. For the fans, there was the added luxury of knowing who each player on the field was by having his name stamped right on the back of his jersey. Fifty years earlier, Pop Warner had the idea of putting numbers on jerseys. The AFL was also the first pro league to make the electric scoreboard clock the official time.

The first game we ever worked in the American Football League was on the night of July 31, 1960, in Kezar Stadium, San Francisco, between the Dallas Texans (now the Kansas City Chiefs) and the Oakland Raiders. Dallas won 20-13. I remember when I first walked into the sparsely filled stadium, I thought, "I hope they didn't print too many programs." It was cold, miserable and foggy. The game films showed us disappearing into and reappearing out of the fog. If the word about the league wasn't strong enough to get people to come out and see us, then the fog was the best place for us to play.

We played an exhibition game in Sacramento, California, between the Oakland Raiders and the Titans (now the New York Jets) and we couldn't even give away our complimentary tickets. Each official was given two tickets to give to friends, relatives, or people we met along the way.

This practice is also done in the National Football League. In the beginning of the American Football League, sometimes we would give the tickets back to the front office or the man at the ticket gate, because we couldn't find anyone to give them to. Things have changed. Sometimes it seems like you just can't win. I remember once I was walking into the Coliseum in Los Angeles to work a college game and some guy from my hometown yelled through the fence to ask me if I had a couple of extra tickets. I told him, "No, in fact, I had to buy a couple extra for my two kids." That was true. Later I discovered that he told everybody he had seen me over at the Coliseum and I had plenty of tickets but wouldn't give him any. I learned a long time ago if I hear someone calling my name when I'm walking into a stadium to keep walking and not pay any attention. Once I am inside, if I hear someone call me, I'll look to see who it is and wave or say hello if there is time. Friends who are inside the stadium already have tickets!

In the first year of the AFL there were a number of players who were free agents, having played out their string in the NFL. Some of the AFL clubs signed them as players but they knew that part of their job was to help teach the rookies about pro football. They were referred to as "retreads." A number of these retreads got the idea that they were going to punch and kick their way through this new, upstart league. The officials had another idea. During that first year I kicked fifteen players out of games, for playing something other than football. In the next thirteen years that I officiated pro ball, I didn't kick out more than five players, total. One particular player, that first year, I kicked out of two games. He didn't last through the first quarter in each contest. Prior to the third game he came over to me and asked if I "had it in for him." I said, "No. As a matter of fact, I'd like to see you play a whole game, but you can't keep slugging and kicking people and stay in this league." He didn't kick or slug anybody that day and after the game he came up to me and asked, "How did I do?" "You did just great. I am proud of you. And so are the guys you didn't beat the hell out of."

In the beginning of the AFL there were only eight teams. The officiating crews were made up of men who came from the same general area. My crew was made up of men from California with the exception of Chuck Liley from Denver. The second year, 1961, Ben Dreith, also from Denver, was switched to our crew to replace Liley. We were known as the Hollywood crew. We worked games that were in the western part of the country. Most of them were in Oakland, San Diego or Denver. We went a long time without going east of Dallas, Houston or Kansas City. When we started going farther east it was usually on a double swing, like a Saturday game in Miami and a Sunday game in Buffalo. With the present schedule in the NFL, an official might work in the same city only once in two or three years. That's a great way to have it. In 1964 we worked three consecutive home exhibition games in Oakland, had two of their games on the road, skipped a week, and returned to their home field the following week to open their regular season play against the Kansas City Chiefs. My crew worked so often in Oakland I was afraid they would award me a "Block O" at the end of the season. On September 27, the day of the Kansas City game, I was standing in the end zone waiting for the television people to let me know when to start the kickoff. I happened to glance over to the Chiefs' coach, Hank Stram. He was pointing at me and holding his nose. I wondered what that was all about until Frank Kirkland, our field judge, pointed behind me. I looked and there was a bunch of fans holding a long piece of butcher paper that said 'WELCOME HOME, BIG JOHN, WE LOST LAST WEEK.'

As officials from the West Coast, one of the things we had to deal with was being accused of favoring western teams in eastern stadiums. Another concern then was that the entire crew rode on the same airplane. What if the plane got diverted, ran into bad weather, or heaven help us, crashed? When the leagues merged, the NFL changed things so that a crew was not made up of officials who came from the same area. This reduced the potential travel problems. If a plane with an official aboard is grounded by a snowstorm there will be enough officials to run the game. I've heard the comment that if the officials don't show, the people will be understanding, but I don't buy that. If one of the teams doesn't show, the people will be understanding. You can't play the game without the other team, but if the officials don't show the people will want to know why the league doesn't have an extra set of men waiting to get on the field. The idea of having two crews of officials on hand would be economically unfeasible. Figure it out. Twenty-eight teams, fourteen games, and seven officials each game. One of the biggest expenses of the NFL is the employment and transportation of officials. Double that cost to have an extra set of officials at each game? Go ahead! What would happen if a game is scheduled and none of the officials showed?

⬥

Prior to a college game years ago I went up to Coach Ben Schwartz-walder of Syracuse and asked him if he was going to do anything out of the ordinary, or different, that my staff ought to know about. He said he didn't plan to, but when I started to walk away he said, "Wait a minute. If you get in the way of one of my players, be a blocker instead of a tackler. Last week one of the officials got in the way and knocked one of our ball carriers down. If it hadn't been for him we would have scored a touchdown." I said, "I don't like to block or tackle anymore. I try to stay out of the way." He said, "O. K., but if you're in the way, be a blocker, don't be a tackler."

I once asked Coach Paul Brown if there was anything unusual his team would do that premature judgment on our part might spoil. He said, "No, nothing. Just straight football. We hope we're good enough to win." And then on the very first play from scrimmage he ran a triple reverse for a touchdown. It had me jumping around like a disco dancer. After the conversion I came by Coach Brown on the sidelines and asked him, "You didn't think that was an unusual play?" He smiled and said, "I forgot to tell you about that one."

Most officials will not talk to a coach who isn't courteous and respectful when he asks questions, protests or hyperactively complains. The best-selling dictionary might be compiled of all the obscene terms that have been contrived on the sidelines and thrown at officials in the quest for unlimited abuse.

A coach might be screaming at one official during an entire game and the official won't hear a word. He can tune him out completely. He has to. A coach might yell and worry himself into such a nervous trance or stupor that the next day, or even after the game, he won't be able to tell you one thing that he said to anybody during the game. There are just a few times when the rules require officials to talk to coaches:

1. At the two-minute warning to find out who their captains are and tell them how many time-outs they have remaining.

2. To give notification of a disqualified player.

3. To shorten the game or remaining periods due to darkness or some other extreme emergency.

4. To give notification that his allowable three time-outs in the half have been taken.

Other than these instances, the designated captains are the sole representatives for their team in communications with officials. Officials will talk to coaches to keep order or game control, and also to clarify some point about the rules. But it is a courtesy. It's none of this talk to the talker, on demand. If officials started listening to advice from coaches and players while the game was going on, we'd all be in trouble. I never minded listening to suggestions after a game about changing a particular ruling. In fact, I have been in favor of some of the ideas coaches have come up with. However, when I get into a game, I am almost completely oblivious to the nervous complaining that comes from coaches and players in the bench area. There aren't too many of them who know the rules and their nuances like the officials do. Coaches know strategies and manipulations of players. Who to keep, who to play here, and who not to play there. When to do this, and when not to. But they don't have the same perspective of the rules and the game we have. The assumptions players make about what is right and what should be right in the rules are often filled with misconceptions.

One coach made a cordial, quiet and sincere attempt to learn on the job and his attempt was dealt with full official hospitality. On January 29, 1966, George Wilson was hired as the first coach of the Miami Dolphins in the American Football League. He had compiled a record of 57-45- 6 as head coach of the NFL Detroit Lions over an eight-year span. George did a fine job of starting his new team with a firm foundation, a team that later became one of the great teams in NFL history. He must have worked twenty hours a day for five and a half months to get ready to coach Miami's first game ever on August 6, 1966. It was a preseason game in San Diego, which the Dolphins lost 38-10. I was the referee of that first game and midway through the second quarter Coach Wilson showed me a lot of class just after a Charger defensive back intercepted a Dolphin pass and took it into the end zone for a touchdown. About halfway through his run the defender dropped the ball, it hit on its flat side, bounced up and the man caught it and went in for the score.

After the conversion, Aaron Wade, our line judge, told me Coach Wilson wanted to talk to me. I went over to him and he said, "I'm new in the AFL. Do your rules allow a player to pick up a fumble and run with it, like the NFL?" I answered "Yes, coach, just like the NFL." He replied, "Thank you, I was just checking." He was a new coach in the

AFL and that fine point in the rules hadn't come up, so he was smart enough to find out right then in a gentlemanly way. He was my kind of coach.

I have spoken to a number of officials' groups and clinics all over the country and the most important point I want to get across to them, especially the young guys, is that officials are the only ones out there on the field who are getting paid to keep their "cool."

"One of the things you should never do is lose your composure, no matter how bad things get. You are the guys who have to keep everything under control." I've never heard of an owner of a ball club fining his coach for yelling at his players because he got all excited. I've never heard of a coach fining or suspending any one of his players because they got all excited and started screaming at people. He wants them excited because it's a very emotional type of game and he wants them up for it.

But an official? Absolutely not. The wilder and hairier it gets, the more composed he has to be. If a guy wants to be a top official, he has to know how to keep his "head" when everything around him is falling apart. I have been known to get mad in a game, but it was strictly for effect. I felt at that particular time that I needed to do it to get game control. There have been times when it was tough to keep from laughing at the shocked look in the players' and coaches' eyes.

During the preseason there's a lot of everything. A lot of fouls are called because players are "overplaying" in an effort to make the team. A lot of fans are upset because they've been forced to buy tickets to all of the preseason games if they want the option to buy their regular season tickets. A lot of players are on the sidelines, sometimes maybe twice as many as there are for the regular season games. And a lot of letters are sent by front row fans to the league office telling them to keep the sidelines clear so that the close sitting fans can see the game. We usually got a memo telling us to try to keep the crowded sidelines clean. I was on a plane going to the Dallas at Philadelphia game in 1970 when I thought of a solution to the sideline problem. Barry Brown asked me about it and I told him I would let him know during the game when I would use it. The answer came early in the first period. The linesman usually takes care of sideline problems. David Hawk, our linesman, had told the players to get back, away from the field. They did, but on the next play they jumped back to see what was happening on the field. A Dallas player had just turned the corner and was tackled and knocked back a few yards. The whole Dallas team was up and pointing to the place where they thought the ball should be spotted which was where the linesman was going to place it anyway. Officials aren't out there asking for anybody's help. Somehow the crowd got the idea the Dallas team had conned him into placing the ball where it didn't belong, and they started to boo. I looked over to Barry and said, "Here it comes." I went over to the Dallas sideline and even surprised myself with how much energy and emphasis I put into it. "All right, everybody, get back. Get back and sit down! You have to keep this area clear. Coach Landry and I have a job to do and we've got to keep it clear so I can see him and he can see me. So, get back and stay there!" The coach turned around and told them all to get back, sit down and stay there. They did, and never got back up again. I turned to Barry and we both smiled. "You conned them. You really conned them," he said. "I didn't con anybody," I said, "but I gotta think of something new next time."

There was a time in pro football when a team was charged a time-out if the trainers came on the field for an injured player. This was to keep teams from taking advantage of calling a player injured when in effect they just wanted more time for player-coach conferences. If a trainer or doctor came onto the field it was considered an official team time-out and after three in one half, a team would be penalized five yards for every additional time-out, whether it was for an injury or not. To keep their team from being charged with a time-out each time a trainer or doctor came onto the field, players began to haul injured players off the field. Now, if an official sees an injured player, he will stop the clock and beckon a trainer or doctor. These two people are the only ones who can touch, administer aid, or direct anyone to do anything to the injured player. The injured player must leave the game and the clock will not start until that player's replacement takes the field. I feel this is better for the game because it protects all players.

In one game, Coach Erdelatz kept coming on the field every time there was an injured player. I cured him of that in a hurry when I stopped the clock after his third visit, and charged Oakland with a time-out. When I did, the Oakland captain, center Jim Otto, asked why I charged them a time out. "Your trainer is out on the field," I told him. "That's not the trainer. That's the head coach," Otto said. "When he comes out on the field to help an injured player, he's the trainer." Otto ran to the coach and said, "Hey, coach, stay off the field, you're using up our time-outs." From that time on, Coach Erdelatz stayed off the field.

## There's Enough Trouble for Everybody

In an All Star game in the Oakland Coliseum, we had some trouble. Down about the five-yard line, up to about the fifteen, on one end of the field, there was a big puddle. It was deep enough that I was afraid some players would drown. And the last thing I wanted to do was give one of those big guys mouth to mouth when he's all full of fertilizer and mud.

We were coming up to the last part of the game when big, great big, Ernie Ladd, 320, 6'11", 17 1/2 EEEE shoes walked over to me and said, "Hey, Big John. I lost my shoe." He's calling me big and I am talking to his navel. "Where'd you put it?" I asked. "It's in there somewhere."

"Oh, hell. Play without it. The game's almost over." A couple of plays later we lost the football. There was a fumble, a big pileup, but no ball. I called time-out and started peeling guys off and when I got to the bottom I didn't have the ball. "All right. Everyone show me your hands," I demanded. I thought they were trying to put something over on me, because it was only an All Star game. There I was with the biggest kids in the world, trying to find out who was the bad boy. I looked down and saw something with a lace going through it, and dug it out. I wasn't even sure it was the ball we were playing with. They asked whose ball it was and I said the West had it last and still has it. And on the next play Daryle Lamonica hit Rod Sherman with an eighty-two yard bomb for a touchdown.

Right before the kickoff is an anxious time. The teams are finishing their last minute instruction with their psyching up hands and voices. Officials are refining their calm, intent upon making sure the show starts well. The fanfare of the opening whistle, the two teams coming at each other, the unedited edition of America's truth Sunday readies itself for the most watched and scrutinized of national rites. There have been both intentional and unintentional exceptions to the ceremonies running smoothly.

Our crew was working a game in Houston when Pete Beathard was playing for the Oilers. Both Frank Kirkland, our field judge, and I knew Pete from his days as a player for the University of Southern California.

At the start of the game the Oilers were ready to kick off. I was down under the receiver's goal post, getting ready to signal for the beginning of the game. I looked at each official for "his" ready signal, a raised hand over his head, but Frank was on the sideline in front of the Oilers' bench. He was talking on a phone. Just as I was going to signal the place kicker to wait, Frank angrily threw the phone down on the AstroTurf behind him. He then raised his hand, and I started the game. At the first time out, I asked him, "What the hell was going on with you and the telephone?" He said just as he was about to give me the "ready" signal, Pete Beathard tapped him on the shoulder with one of the field phones and said, "Telephone call from Long Beach, California, Frank." Frank said, "I thought, my God, something terrible has happened at home and I grabbed the phone and said, 'Hello, hello, this is Frank Kirkland!!" The voice on the other end said, "Yes, we know. We can see you, Frank. This is the Oilers' scouting booth in the top of the stadium."

⬥

The referee has complete control of what happens on that field. He is in effect the complete policeman. He has to be. A photographer, at a game I worked at San Bernardino's Orange Show Stadium, came onto the field after a touchdown was scored and screamed, "He didn't score! He didn't score! I got it on film. You can't score that TD, I got it on film!"

"What do you think this is, a horse race? Get off the field. We don't use any photo finishes," I told him 'gently.'

He still wanted to argue. A cop was standing nearby and I waved him over. When he came I told him, "Take him clear out of the stadium. I mean clear out to the street."

As the officer was escorting him out, he yelled back, "I am a newspaperman."

"Well you just lost the privilege of being inside. You should have been in the press box, anyway."

The old time officials tell me that in the early days of pro football, it was a poor paying, part time job for players and officials. Each team carried along its own "policeman," a player delegated to keep members of the other team from harming the men on his team. Any unsportsmanlike conduct, and the "officer" would exact comprehensive punishment on those who wronged. As far as I know there are no longer policemen in the game. We have taken their place, and the roughest we ever get is to separate the guys who are going to extremes with each other, and make sure disobedience is paid for with the loss of land, not limb.

You need a lot of fast retorts when players or coaches give you a hard time in their rapid critiquing of your work. Such compliments as:

"Hey, ref, why don't you get your head in the game?"

and

"Straighten up, ref, you're missing a great game."

I usually ignore them or come back with a few one liners like, "Why, thank you very much. I've had good football players (coaches) say the same thing," or "Gee, they thought it was a good call on the other bench." The safest comment of all, though, is to just tell them, "If they do the same thing, don't worry, I'll call it on them."

I never got too upset when a player who had made a mistake and caused a foul went around trying to lay the blame on someone else. I just figured he was looking out for his best interests. Of course, there was a limit to how much he could say and when he could say it. As a matter of fact, officials do players a favor by ignoring the verbal blasts. If we paid too much attention, we would wind up having to penalize them to regain game control.

Bob Austin, who was the first Supervisor of Officials in the American Football League, used to tell us that if a player calls you something in the heat of battle, nothing extreme and just between the two of you, it's up to you to come back with a fast answer and calm him down. You don't have to throw him out of the game or throw a flag on him. But if he starts to malign you in front of the troops and the other players and you feel you could lose game control, then you have to stop him with something that affects him and his team. Then the flag comes out.

Warnings to players about minor mistakes they are making can be done without causing any bias; in fact, players and coaches appreciate them. I am talking about someone who may be lining up a few inches offside, or be a tiny bit into the back edge of the ball. He can be warned but only once. The next time he does it, he gets called for it.

You might see an official talking to a player on the field after a play and the official could be telling him, in reaction to the last play, "If you had grabbed him it would have been holding," or "If you had hit him you might not be in the game."

The clipping fouls, the striking fouls, anything unsportsmanlike, have to be called every time. One of the marks of a good official is if he can differentiate between the warning offenses and those that must always be called.

Let's say an umpire sees someone on offense who hasn't done anything wrong yet, but he's starting to grab at people, so he's getting close to holding. All that official has to say is, "Smith, keep your hands in." Right away it registers with Smith that, "he knows my name and he's watching." This kind of "preventive officiating" can help to keep the game from being spoiled by a lot of fouls. Calling out the player's name is effective for it makes the warning more direct and personal. The names on the backs of the players' jerseys is a great help in this department.

In pro football the guy you're playing against may have been your roommate last week. He may have been the guy you played with in high school or college. Two players pitted against each other might have been talked about in the press the preceding week. Players may even be bitter rivals, unprovoked by the news media. Whatever the circumstances, discussions between and among the players on the field can and do go on.

Whenever the talk gets on the serious side, an official can keep game control by moving in between plays and saying to the players involved, "Hey, let's knock off the chatter. This is a football game, not a debate."

What I used to do when it looked like it might turn into something more serious was to talk to the players individually. While the offensive team was in the huddle I'd call out the name of the defensive player and say, "Hey, Jim, he's getting to you. He's making you play his game. Don't let him get to you. Keep your cool," and walk away.

Then, as I walked past the huddle or after the next play, I would tell the offensive player the same thing.

When players complain to officials that another player is shoving them or pushing off on them, officials will usually say, "I'll take a look."

Officials tend to respect players who don't have the reputation for being criers. Usually if a player sees the man he is playing against go over to an official and it looks like he is complaining, it's almost certain that for the next couple of plays he won't do whatever it may be that he is being accused of. Players might feel after they complain about another player the official will devote all of his attention to that player, but that's not how it works.

The official has specific places that he must watch. These are the areas he has to concentrate on and he can't spend all of his energies looking at one player until he catches him in the act.

In the Minnesota-San Diego preseason game of 1971, both benches emptied onto the field to join in the fighting and each player was assessed a healthy fine by the commissioner for leaving the bench and getting into the melee. The fines, however, were subsequently dropped and the monies returned to the players because the league had never bargained with the Players' Association concerning the invoking of a fine for coming off the bench to join in a fight.

The year after I retired, I ran into Bum Phillips, who at the time of the fight was an assistant coach of the San Diego Chargers, and is now the head coach of the Houston Oilers. While we were having lunch, Bum told me that the San Diego owner had paid the fines for his players and later when the league returned the fines to each player, according to the court order, only one or two players sent their fine back to the owner. So, in effect, each San Diego player got a bonus for getting into a fight.

I remember another fight where both benches emptied onto the field. Both benches were on the same side of the field. The game film zeroed in on two guys who were running towards the fight, one from each bench. One of them had his helmet on and the other one didn't. The one with his helmet on turned toward the other guy and yelled and the guy with his helmet off laughed and put his helmet on, and they both ran to the edge of the fight and started pushing each other. They were probably former roommates before one or both of them got traded. One thing a player should remember is, "Never take your helmet off in a fight."

## Paid to Decide

Another time I earned my money well was on Sunday, October 1, 1972, when the Washington Redskins were playing the New England Patriots in Foxboro, Massachusetts. Up until this time in the season the Redskins hadn't lost a game and the Patriots had won one and lost one. It came down to the end of the game with about 1:03 left on the clock and Washington kicked a field goal to tie the score at 24 to 24. Unfortunately, a Patriot end ran into the kicker and I threw a flag on him and everybody in Boston was ready to hang me. Now the Redskins had a choice. They could leave it 24-24 and take the penalty on the next kickoff or they could set the score back to 21-24, take the penalty which would give them a first down on the eighteen-yard line. The strategy is that they can run three plays and if they don't score a touchdown they can still kick a field goal and tie it up again.

George Allen, the Redskins' coach, made the only choice he really had and the Redskins took possession. Well, they ran three plays and missed the field goal attempt. There were about thirty seconds left on the clock, and in came the offensive team from Boston. We put the ball on the twenty because a missed field goal from inside the twenty is a touchback. The Pats had the ball first and ten on the twenty going out. Jim Plunkett, who played at Stanford with my son, came running by me and said, "That's the greatest call you ever made, John."

"Yeah, but they didn't think so a few minutes ago."

The Pats ran three plays and didn't make their first down. There were four seconds left on the clock and they had to kick. The Redskins blocked the kick and the ball rolled across the end zone. Just as it rolled out, the guy that blocked it tried to fall on it. He never really controlled it, but he rolled over the top of it and out of bounds. But, a split second before he fell on the ball, his own end came sliding in on the wet surface to scoop it in. He touched the football just as both of his feet were touching the end line.

The rule says that a loose ball touched by a player or anything else, in contact with, or outside of a boundary line is immediately dead and out of bounds.

As he touched the ball he was out of bounds, which made the ball out of bounds. He caused it to be out of bounds and it was a two-point safety for Washington making it 24-23 ending in favor of New England. I gave the signal for a safety, both palms together over my head, and moved President Nixon off the front page of the Washington Post for the whole week.

The Kansas City Chiefs were playing the Denver Broncos. Kansas City scored just before the half to put them within three points of the Broncos. Four seconds were left in the half when they kicked off to the Broncos. It was an onside kick and a Kansas City player recovered it. He could not advance it because his team kicked it.

By rule, the clock did not start when Kansas City legally recovered their own kick. A league rule at that time was that during the last two minutes of a half, the clock didn't start after a kickoff until the referee signaled, "ready for play." The rule has since been changed so that the clock starts on the snap of the ball. One of the Denver players, I believe it was the middle guard, smacked through the line just after I put the ball in play, causing a five-yard penalty for encroachment, just as the clock ran down to zero. I marked off the penalty. Because it was a defensive foul on the last down of the half, Kansas City got an extra play. And, on that play Kansas City kicked a field goal, right through the uprights. Denver fans went wild as the score-board showed no time left and the game tied.

A Denver sportswriter was outside the official's dressing room along with league commissioner Joe Foss. Joe gave me permission to talk with the writer who wanted me to explain what had happened; how time is handled in the last two minutes, and other advice I could give him on how to calm down an irate populace who thought they had their victory given away by a bad or fast call. Not too many people, it seemed, were aware that the clock didn't start when a team legally recovered its own kick, and that a foul by the defense, when time runs out on a play, automatically gives the offense another play, free of a foul by the defense.

In the beginning of the AFL, Buffalo was playing Houston. Buffalo had a chance to make the playoffs. Houston didn't. We were going into the closing minutes of the game and Buffalo was ahead by a few points and had possession of the ball near the Houston twenty-five yard line. It was third down with a few yards to go. They had come out of the huddle and I had started the thirty-second count with the field judge. The quarterback started calling signals and all of a sudden the field judge blew his whistle, threw his flag in the air, and gave the signal for "delay," which meant they had exceeded the thirty-second count. Now on a de-lay foul you don't need to ask the captain, you just pick up the ball, walk off the five yards, give the signal, and get on with the game. As I leaned over to pick up the ball, I glanced at the clock behind me and saw 1:58 left in the game, which meant one of two things:

1. The field judge did not stop the game at two minutes because he was thinking of the thirty-second count, or

2. The timekeeper had let the clock slide over a few seconds and the thirty seconds was up at say 2:01 or 2:02.

I asked the field judge if he was sure it was for delay and he yelled back to me, "Delay! Delay!" So I marched off the five yards, then gave the teams the two-minute warning.

Buffalo went back into the huddle, probably changed their strategy and came out with a pass play. It was intercepted. Houston took over with that old retreaded quarterback who everybody thought was over the hill, George Blanda. He took his team down with passes:

zip—out of bounds

zip—out of bounds

time out

zip—out of bounds.

He moved his team to the other end of the field, hit a receiver in the end zone and scored with just a few seconds left and won.

After the game the field judge came into the dressing room and told me he blew the foul, that he should have called time out for the two-minute warning and not delay of the game. Ralph Wilson, the owner of the Bills, went right through the roof, and rightly so.

The next morning I got a call from Thurlo McCrady, Supervisor of Officials, who wanted to know what had happened. I explained it to him and then wrote out a report which stated that one of the prime duties of the field judge was to keep the time, that I had checked with him and that a mistake had definitely been made.

I suffered with this whole thing for a week. The media got hold of it. One writer for the Los Angeles Times even closed one of his columns by saying that it looked as if five officials would loose their stripes. To make things worse, I had the next weekend off. During the broadcast of a game that Sunday, an announcer said on television that Buffalo owner Ralph Wilson had demanded that all officials of the Buffalo Houston game be fired.

That would do it. I figured I was on my way out. The next day, I got a call from Thurlo and he said there would be some fines levied and that the field judge was no longer in the league. I got a letter from commissioner Joe Foss, and sent in a $125 fine. As luck would have it, I was assigned the Buffalo-Denver game for the following Sunday.

The Denver stadium had two clocks and the only one that Buffalo could see malfunctioned. The Buffalo coach yelled at me about it. I stopped the game to find out from the timer what was wrong. He told me that the clock couldn't be fixed.

I told the coach that we would tell him the official time remaining in the game after each play. "It will come from the head linesman, who is right in front of you. We'll yell it to him and he'll yell it to you."

I found out later that Mr. Wilson had called Thurlo the following day to tell him what a fine job he thought the referee did in improvising through the broken clock situation. Thurlo told him I was the same referee who had worked the game two weeks before.

All the guys on the crew thought the fine wasn't fair, but none of them thought enough about it to kick in some money to help me pay it.

Late in the season, the incident turned full circle. After one of the postseason playoff games, Joe Foss came up to me. When he shook my hand I felt some paper. At first I thought it was notice that I wouldn't be working in the league for the following year. Not quite. It was the money I had paid for the fine. So far as I have been able to find out, no other official has ever been fined, but they have been suspended. When you're suspended from a game or two for a mistake, it's the same as being fined.

I made a mistake once by taking something for granted. After every score, the referee must ask the captain of the team scored upon if he wants to kick or receive. One in a thousand times, on a windy, rainy day, he might decide to kick. This caused me some embarrassment at Balboa Stadium in San Diego.

As soon as the kicking team kicked the extra point, I turned and ran to the far end of the field to get ready for the kickoff. When I got there I turned around and I suddenly realized that I should be at the other end of the field, one hundred yards away, under the receiving team's goal post. Instead, there I was thirty yards behind the kicking team, looking at their backs.

I didn't dare blow the whistle because the kicker would kick off. Instead, I yelled, "Wait a minute." He turned and gave me a puzzled look as I ran by him.

"Don't kick the ball until I signal you from the other end of the field."

The stadium was filled and there was a large TV audience, not to mention the incredulous members of my crew. Everyone waited while

I ran a one hundred yard solo all the way down to the other end of the field. As a cover up to those who might have asked questions about what I was doing, I first ran over to the TV coordinator on the sidelines to make it look like the delay was caused by television.

I even acted out the part asking him, "Are you ready?"

Surprised, he answered, "We've been ready for quite a while, John." I sprinted down to stand under the goal post and then signaled for the kickoff.

After the game, my boss, Thurlo McCrady, said, "You were really busy checking things out down there before that kickoff. What was the delay for?" I earned most of the money I got paid that day 'talking' myself off the hook.

I am not saying that officials don't miss calls or make some errors in officiating mechanics. I will always remember though, what I heard the late coach Red Sanders of UCLA say after a game I officiated. He answered a question from a reporter who asked his feelings about the officiating of the game, and with his very droll sense of humor he said, "Well, gentlemen, I'll tell ya. There's three elements in a ball game. There's the players and there's the coaches and there's the officials. And, if I can ever get my players and my coaches to make as few mistakes as the officials, there ain't nobody who's ever going to beat us. Any more questions?"

Games have been stopped for impossible fan behavior, fighting, delays for television and the ritual of a triumphant gallop of horses onto the side of the field when a team scored, but I was working a game that stopped for the most beautiful reason of all, a tribute to a player.

It was during a preseason game at the Los Angeles Coliseum. Lamar Lundy, a great defensive end with the Rams, and a member of their famous "Fearsome Foursome," had been painfully stricken with myasthenia gravis, which causes deterioration of the muscles. It frequently totally immobilizes its victim and is often fatal. I didn't know Lamar had been wheeled into the Coliseum until the announcer, John Ramsey, told the fans after a scoring play that downfield, behind the western end zone, was one of the greatest Rams of all times, Lamar Lundy.

When the spotlight shined on him, the crowd stood up and cheered and cheered for at least five minutes. I had to hold up the game. I didn't have any control. I didn't even want it. The people wanted to give him their tribute and stopped the game to do so. A number of the players ran down and shook hands with him and patted him on the shoulders and there were a lot of wet eyes for a while in the stadium.

I know that the rest of the Fearsome Foursome, Merlin Olsen, Deacon Jones, and Rosey Grier, did a lot to help raise funds for him and for the fight against myasthenia gravis. One of those programs was the L.A. Chapter of Myasthenia Gravis Foundation Salute to the Fearsome Foursome on January 21, 1978 in Los Angeles. Lamar Lundy was on his way back, not to pro football, but to a productive life.

One of the most inspiring games I ever worked was one between the Raiders and the Chiefs, played at the University of Washington, in Seattle. The proceeds of that game were for Brian Sternberg, a pole vaulter who had become handicapped through a freak trampoline accident. During the halftime many athletes competed in a mini track meet. Some of them talked to Brian through an intercom on the field. It was an emotional moment when Brian told them how great it was that they were out there competing for him, doing what he could no longer do.

I was in San Francisco and saw the 49ers play the Rams in a pre-season game of the 1977 football season. When Joe Namath came into the game the crowd gave him a big hand. This guy was one of the greats and they wanted him to know how much they appreciated him. But you should have heard the fans cheer when he got sacked by the 49er defensive line. This is one thing about pro football that makes it different from other levels of the game. The fans can show their class for a player's ability no matter who he plays for.

Fans don't get a complete picture of Joe. His image is so often pumped out of proportion, the human side of him gets lost.

When the Jets were going to Miami to play Baltimore in Super Bowl III, he said they would beat Baltimore. Hardly anyone else thought that was possible.

The Jets had four equipment boys and when Joe walked into the dressing room the kids were packing the gear into the big trunks to go to Miami. One of the kids was in tears. Joe asked him what was wrong and the kid said, "They're only gonna take three of us and we flipped and I lost. I can't go."

"I guess they don't understand how much the guys on the team appreciate what you do for us all year. Here," he gave the boy three one hundred dollar bills. "You get yourself a plane ticket and you come to Miami with us and keep track of your expenses and let me know if it costs you any more for the trip." You don't always hear about those kinds of things that he does, but that's the kind of guy he is.

One of my favorite football stories is about a tribute paid to Joe. Our crew had just finished working the Kansas City-Pittsburgh game on November 15, 1970, and had a two-hour delay at the Pittsburgh airport. We were sitting in the airline hospitality room, watching the Rams-Jets telecast from the West Coast. Joe had suffered a fractured right wrist in the Baltimore game three weeks earlier and was out for the season. The Jets had been struggling along ever since. Sitting with us, with a large cigar clamped between his teeth was a priest, who just happened to be six feet six and weighed about three hundred pounds.

A lady came into the room and asked, "Who's playing?"

"The Rams and the Jets," someone said.

"What quarter is it?" she asked.

"The fourth," I answered.

"What's the score?"

"31-20. The Jets are winning."

"You mean the Jets are beating the Rams and they're doing it without Namath?"

"Who's playing quarterback?" her husband asked.

"Jesus," the priest said dramatically, as he stuffed his cigar back into his mouth.

## We've proven to officials we don't love the human element, we don't excuse their mistakes, and won't let them repent.

—*Sport Joys and Gifts of Play,* by Paul T. Owens

Any official who tells me he's never blown an inadvertent whistle is either lying, fooling himself, or both. I'm not sure I want him working with me because he apparently doesn't have the in-depth knowledge, or feel for the game that will keep him constantly alert to blowing one. One of the last things I said in every final pregame conference was, "Remember, don't hit your whistle unless you actually see the ball become dead in the possession of the player."

Instant replays can help in some situations, but not with an inadvertent whistle. The replay will show you what happened after the whistle, but by the dictates of the rule book, that action has no bearing on the play because everything that happens after the whistle sounded is on a dead ball, the play has ended. If human beings didn't blow whistles that stop plays, all the players would run the risk of very serious injury. There is no machine capable of following the moves of a wide receiver that can signal the other twenty-one players, "The ball is dead, stop the action."

Rule 7, Section 4, Article 1, of the NFL rule book covers the fifteen ways in which a ball becomes dead and the down is ended. Paragraph (n) states:

"When any official signals dead ball or sounds his whistle, even though inadvertently, the ball is dead."

I think most owners and coaches, when they stop and really think about it, would tell you that they would much rather have a rare inadvertent whistle than a busted up ball player.

The official who blows an unintentional whistle feels as rotten about it as a receiver feels about the pass that he dropped in the end zone, or as badly as the field goal kicker feels about the second straight game-losing kick he missed. The player has many chances to redeem himself, but the official who blows an inadvertent whistle must live with the horror of it for the rest of his life.

There are basically two types of inadvertent whistles. One occurs when the quarterback fakes so well that he not only fools the defense, but the officials as well. The whistle is blown on the faker instead of the taker. But no matter how far the runner gets, the ball is dead where the ball was when the whistle was blown. It's a left-handed compliment to the quarterback for keeping everybody in the dark, except for his teammates. With seven officials in the pro ranks, this type of inadvertent whistle rarely occurs.

The second type of misblown whistle is the one that is sounded after the ball is fumbled.

We went back to work a game between Atlanta and Minnesota in Bloomington on November 28, 1972. It was just before halftime and Minnesota had the ball on Atlanta's seven or eight-yard line. The next play Minnesota opened a wide gap and went straight through to score a touchdown. On that play, just as the guy with the ball crossed the five-yard line, a whistle sounded. Right away I am thinking one of my guys blew an inadvertent whistle. I looked at my officials and they all looked stunned. Harry Kessel, our head linesman, was signaling "touchdown" when I suddenly realized what had happened. A high school band was standing there ready to go on the field for the halftime entertainment. I figured immediately that the drum major had hit his whistle to bring his band to attention. I ran straight up to him, grabbed his whistle in my hand, shook my finger in his face and told him, "Don't you blow this thing again 'til halftime." His eyes popped out like pingpong balls. "Yes sir! Yes sir!"

I ran back onto the field and as I passed one of the Atlanta players, he said, "Hey, one of your guys blew a whistle."

"No, he didn't. It was the drum major of that band."

"Okay," he said. Thank God I saw the kid and the whistle and connected them together; otherwise we could have had a protest that looked like a filibuster in the United States Senate. Nothing can cause more problems to both teams than for somebody to get a whistle and bring it to the game and start making their own game calls. This can really hurt the game and particularly the players.

We were once down in San Diego, and deep into the third quarter, when a self-appointed official started blowing his whistle in the middle of every play when the visiting team had the ball. It confused the hell out of everybody. Captains were complaining and finally I just stopped the clock. I went over to the sideline phones and called the public address announcer and told him to announce that both captains have requested that the person blowing the whistle in the stands please refrain from doing so, as it was confusing to both teams. The public address announcer spoke out abruptly, "Your attention please! The referee has ordered that the person in the stands blowing the whistle stop blowing it or he will penalize San Diego." The entire place suddenly sounded like

Birdland, U.S.A. People must have gone out and bought whistles and brought them in. It was chaos for the rest of the game.

A few weeks later at another game, there was a similar situation. A fan in the stands started blowing a whistle, just before the half. When we went down to the officials' dressing room at halftime I telephoned up to the press box and asked to speak to the public address announcer. When he got on the phone, I said, "Now, I am going to tell you something. I want you to write it down and I want you to read it exactly as I have given it to you. I don't want you to add or take away one word." He agreed.

"What do you want me to say?"

"I want you to say, 'Your attention, please. Someone in the stands is blowing a whistle. It is confusing both football teams and it is a dangerous thing to do. The captains and the coaches of both teams have requested that you do not blow the whistle any more. We would appreciate your consideration for everybody on the field. Thank you.'"

I told him not to say anything else and above all not to threaten them. As soon as we came onto the field for the second half the announcer read it exactly as I said and we never heard another whistle out of the crowd. The first way was done with a threat and no one in a crowd wants to abide by that. The second way was by request of the players and coaches and everyone seemed to respect it. If the guy who blew the whistle had done it again, I think the people around him would have clobbered him good.

The films showed it. The fans knew it. They played the instant replay five times so no one could miss it. The coach who was covered with victory champagne knew it, but he accepted all the winning handshakes and hugs.

Letters were written by the losing team's supporters to the papers, to the league, to the world at large, and there was hardly anyone who could deny it. AN INADVERTENT WHISTLE HAD GIVEN THE TEAM THE GAME AND THE PLAYOFFS.

But honey, I thought you loved me and would try to understand;
my heart belongs to the quarterback, I'm his one heart rooting band.

# Protect My Quarterback

A whistle was blown about one hundredth of a second too soon and the play was stopped before the defense could legally recover the fumble. Tough! The same rule book that says a touchdown is worth six points, says when a whistle blows while a ball is loose, it goes back to the team that fumbled it.

Constantly, coaches plead with officials to protect their quarterback. If four linemen had tackled that quarterback and he had been taken out of the game, hurt and unable to play again, it would have been a late whistle instead of a quick one. Maybe the whistle was blown quickly, or inadvertently because the official had his angle of vision blocked. The official could not see when the ball was ripped, squeezed away, or dropped by the quarterback.

John Madden, the Oakland Raiders coach, would always say to me before the game, "Hey, John. Protect my quarterback, will you?"

I'd tell him, "Well, I am not going to block for him. But don't worry, coach. I know all about quarterbacks because my son is one. I am not going to take my eyes off him."

Then, in the middle of the first quarter, his quarterback would throw the ball so late that the defensive linemen couldn't stop themselves from hitting him after he had released the ball.

Then Coach Madden would yell from the sidelines, "Hey, what about my quarterback. . . What about your son?"

"Well, tell him to throw the ball sooner." To this day, every time I see Coach Madden, he reminds me of those times.

It seems that about the middle of each season some quarterback is injured and a team's chances are ruined. When this happens we get an outcry from owners, coaches and the sports media saying, "Protect the quarterback," and "Why aren't quarterbacks afforded the same protection as kickers?"

Well, there are a few very important differences between a quarterback and a kicker. The kicker only has his protection when he keeps his identity as a kicker. If he gets the snap from the center and goes right into his kick, he is protected until he becomes a potential tackler, a time at which he may be legally blocked. If he gets a bad snap and starts to run, he becomes a running back and may be tackled. He only regains his protection if he completely reestablishes himself as a kicker. If he kicks while he is running and gets knocked down, there is no foul, unless in the opinion of the referee he has been unnecessarily roughed.

A quarterback is always a potential runner, and when he starts to scramble, he may be tackled the same as any other runner. If he suddenly stops and throws, or throws while he is running, he can be tackled like any other man who had possession of the ball. If he throws the ball while he is running, in time for the defense to avoid hitting him and they belt him anyway, then they will be called for unnecessary roughness. It's difficult to expect the defense to keep from hitting him after they've been chasing him all over the field. The official decides if they should have been able to stop.

I don't think I've ever called a player for a late hit on a scrambling quarterback or kicker that I didn't get growls out of the defense, telling me that they lost their protection when they started to run. One time, after I made a roughness call, the owner of the team that fouled was so upset that he complained to the supervisor of officials. A week later, his own quarterback scrambled out of the pocket and was hit by two big defensive linemen, just at the split second the ball left his hand. The quarterback was hurt on the play and missed the next four games of the season. The owner was then quoted as saying that something had to be done to protect the quarterbacks. Perhaps he should have talked to his own defensive coach about going after scrambling quarterbacks.

Whenever I hear about a quarterback being hurt, I always want to know what he was doing when he got hit. Was he scrambling or did he hold the ball so long that he released it just as the defensive players were about to hit him? When I was Supervisor of Officials for the World Football League, we had three quarterbacks hurt on the same weekend. The cry went up immediately that the officials weren't protecting them. I checked out each one, and in every case the quarterback was running with the ball, was tackled, and never did throw the ball. They were running backs at the time, and prone to all of the risks every other running back takes.

Maybe we could change the rules to require all quarterbacks to wear polka dot uniforms so that everyone could identify them quickly. The officials could declare the ball dead as soon as anyone on the defense merely touched them. If anyone tackled them it would be a foul. We could make them promise that they would stay in the pocket and pass, and that we would blow the whistle the instant they started to scramble. Maybe we shouldn't allow them to run the ball past the line o scrimmage. These ideas would take most of the thrill out of the game, but they would help protect the physical health of the quarterback.

I am still waiting for the owner or coach, whose team was "hurt" by a quick whistle, to come forward and say, "I find no fault with the official. He protected my opponent's quarterback on that play and there will be a play sometime this season when he'll do the same thing for my quarterback. I'd rather have a healthy quarterback than a receiver fumble, any day."

Joe Namath probably said it better than anybody else, when he pointed out that if the defensive linemen and the linebackers do their job right, they get their prize, "Me."

At the Denver Bronco stadium, after the Big Orange crushes the enemy quarterback, they show a picture on their instant replay scoreboard of a horse opening up a sack and making room for the quarterback to fit in it. When the horse gets him in the sack, he ties the rope to close it and smiles. The fans roar their approval. Besides coming to see their team win, one of the most important reasons to cheer is when the defensive rush puts the quarterback where he belongs—in the sack.

If the fans wrote to the league and said they didn't want to see the sack in the game because of the potential danger to the quarterback, and the owners complained in unison, and if the quarterbacks organized and boycotted games until they were guaranteed that football would be a non-collision sport, then you wouldn't have a coach yelling at a referee to protect his quarterback. And you certainly wouldn't have football edging closer to the first prosthetically thrown touchdown pass.

❦

Coaches can get caught in an emotional trap when they review game films and come up with such a classic statement as, "That call cost us the ball game."

They have the idea that the official actually knew that the call was going to cost them the game. Maybe the call did cost them the ball game, but it wasn't the official who cost them anything. Go find number 68 or number 57 who held on the play that was called back with penalty yardage. That's the cause for the losing game, not the call. The official sees the foul and throws the flag. He isn't aware, nor does he care, if the call he makes is going to be to one team's advantage or not. He has no way of knowing when he throws the flag what may happen in the next split second of play. The team that fouled may throw a pass on the play and the pass may be intercepted and may be run back for a touchdown. Obviously in that case, the scoring team will refuse the penalty and take the touchdown. Now how is an official supposed to know that?

Officials have often been accused of being responsible for an injury, too. People get the idea that if they had called the foul, the gross clip or hold or bad pop wouldn't have happened. The conclusion is that since an official didn't make the call on a play when a player got hurt, that the injury was partly or entirely due to the official. The official had nothing to do with anyone getting hurt. The player who committed the foul is the one who is responsible.

I'll grant you that every official on the field wishes he could have the play over again. He hates to think that a kid got hurt by a foul play and the guy got away with it. That he actually got a cheap shot in and didn't get caught in the act. But it happens and it's going to continue to happen. You can't get them all. There are seven guys out there watching twenty-two players so you're not going to get them all, but somehow people get the idea that if the official had called the foul, that kid wouldn't be in the hospital. He's still going to be in the hospital. Calling the foul wouldn't have prevented the injury.

I had a situation one time where the quarterback was running with the football and got hurt. As I said earlier, he's running, he doesn't have any more protection than any other runner. He's just as vulnerable as a regular running back. Once he throws the ball, he has protection. If he doesn't go out and try and block somebody after he throws the ball, then he has protection because he is still the passer. But until he throws it, he's a runner. Now, here comes a quarterback and he's late. He throws the ball, but he's used up so much of his time back there trying to find an open receiver that the player or players chasing him can't avoid hitting him. The call becomes a judgment one for the referee. Was there roughing the passer?

One time a quarterback was running and it looked like he was going to go forward, past the line of scrimmage and try to run for a gain, then at the last second he found a receiver and fired the ball. Just as he released the ball the defensive player was right up into his chest and crushed him. The lineman's head went right up underneath the quarterback's chin and broke his jaw. (I read later he swallowed two teeth.) No foul called, because I had determined that he had released the ball too late. There were claims by the quarterback's team that the defensive player hit him with the cast he was wearing on his arm, but that wasn't true, it was the top of his head gear that got him. The quarterback was through for the season with his jaw wired shut. The league office backed us up on it. Everyone who saw the films could see that the call was right.

Some of the writers, in discussing the incident, would lead you to believe that if a foul had been called the player wouldn't have been hurt. If there had been a foul and I had called it, the quarterback still would have gone to the hospital. I felt sorry for the player, but the longer the quarterback keeps the ball the greater his jeopardy.

The rule is that when a man is obviously out of the play he can't be tackled or hit. When he's got the ball he's open game. Good linebackers tell you, "My job is to go in there and find the guy with the seed, sort

him out and crunch him." With a job description like that, somebody's bound to go to the hospital once in a while.

Some coaches will run up to an official after the second quarter and yell, shaking their fists and swinging their programs and game plans. Sometimes they do it for the crowd, but I think more often it's just to let off game pressure.

It's the first chance they have to "get on" you without picking up a fifteen-yard penalty. And, as long as they're not violent, or talk to us in an abusive manner, we'll go right along with them. One of the occupational hazards of being an official is being a part time whipping boy for the coaches.

Weeb Eubank, the New York Jets coach, chased me right up to the locker room door once. He wasn't happy either. It was at halftime in a game between the Jets and San Diego Chargers.

That day, October 13, 1963, in San Diego Weeb had good reason to be concerned. Just before the end of the half, New York attempted a thirty-five-yard field goal and the wind carried the ball around the goalposts. It never crossed over the crossbars between the uprights. Weeb thought the ball had gone between the posts. Had I been standing next to him on the sidelines, I'm sure I would have agreed with him. He was irate and blamed me for missing the call because I made it from so far back. At that time, with only five officials, the referee ruled on the success or failure of a field goal, standing behind the kicker.

"Why don't you put two guys down there right under the goal posts and let them look straight up. That way there won't be any kind of guessing about the call. Why are you trying to call it from way back there?" Weeb asked.

"I think you've got a point, Weeb. Tell you what you do. You write to Thurlo McCrady, our supervisor, with the suggestion. I'll put it in my report and ask if my crew can try it in a game. If it works out, we might be able to change the mechanics all over the league."

He wrote the letter and I put it in my report and the following Wednesday I got a call from Thurlo McCrady telling me to work out the mechanics with my crew and try out Weeb's suggestion. We tried it for three weeks and it worked well.

The referee is no longer responsible for looking to see if the ball goes between the uprights. It's now up to the field judge and the back judge, who are standing under the posts with their eyes focused upwards. This system is now the mechanics in all of pro ball, college ball, and many high school leagues. The referee is back to his primary duty of being sure there is no roughing of the kicker or the holder or any illegal blocks to protect them.

The colleges widened the posts to encourage field goal kicking and to improve scoring possibilities. This also started with the coaches. They asked that the goal posts be moved up to the goal line instead of being on the endline, at the back of the end zone.

The NCAA rules committee thought that would create an extra danger so they decided to leave them on the end line but spread the space between the uprights. This widened the area of aim for the place kicker, thus giving him and the offense one more advantage.

A few years later, the pros wanted to discourage the use of the field goal. They changed the kicking rule so that if you missed on an attempted field goal, the other team would get the ball, first and ten, back at the original line of scrimmage, the "previous spot" as football people call it. At the same time they moved their goal posts back to the end of the end zone.

Every year the competition committee of the National Football League considers possible rule changes in a continuing effort to create a balance between offensive and defensive play. They are also interested in any rules that will improve the safety of the game and increase the entertainment value for the fan.

Ken Stabler,
Oakland Raiders
Quarterback

*I was playing for the Patriots in 1960 and got a knee injury. It felt like people were jabbing me with red hot pokers. When the doctor said, "Let's move him," I looked up at you and you looked right at me and said, "Take it easy, son. You're going to be o.k. You'll be back in here." I felt there was one person out there looking out for me.*
—Lee Phelps, Santa Ana, California

Just because officials are precise, accurate and automatic in our work and don't smile, doesn't mean we lack feelings. I have felt damn sorry for players and coaches, and have been touched deeply by tributes given to them by fans.

Keith Lincoln played for the San Diego Chargers for a number of years and then they traded him. After a few years, they traded back for him. I was refereeing the game when Lincoln came back. The stadium was decked out with banners painted:

## WELCOME BACK HONEST ABE, and SAN DIEGO IS LINCOLN COUNTRY

He had only been back a few days so he was used mostly on specialty teams, to return punts, kicks, and kickoffs, and maybe run one or two scrimmage plays. He was standing back by the goalpost ready to receive a kickoff and I said to him, "I guess it's nice to be home."

And he looked around the stadium and said, "How about that. Can you believe these people? Isn't it great of them to come out and give a guy an ovation like this?"

I said it sure was a nice tribute, and by then the television guy had taken his arm down and we were ready for the kickoff. I signaled for play to begin. Keith got the ball, and ran almost to midfield before he was driven out of bounds. As he was hit, one of his legs was caught and twisted by the tackle and pileup. We got everybody else up, but Keith. The doctors came then, and he was taken off the field on a stretcher. It was announced that Keith Lincoln had a broken leg and was out for the season. About a half hour later he was rolled out in a wheelchair with his leg in a cast. There was no way the game could go on. Even the opponents were cheering for the guy. He got a standing ovation and everyone in the stadium was in tears.

There was pathos again on November 12, 1972, when the 49ers were playing Baltimore in Candlestick Park. In this particular game the starting quarterback was shaken up on a play. I was standing there looking down at the young quarterback who was knocked about semi cold. He was all right, but his bell was rung and he was going to have to sit out of the game for a while. I wondered what everyone was cheering about and then I looked over at the Baltimore side of the field and there was the gifted Johnny Unitas warming up to go in for the injured player. The San Francisco fans were letting him know that he was still one of the best there was, even though he was playing against them. But he got blitzed on the very first play. The reaction of the crowd was amazing. The minute he got sacked the place just went wild. It was his only play. He was injured.

When he didn't get up, the crowd went into a deep groan. He sat there on the turf as the team attendants administered to him, and the other quarterback came back into the game. Unitas limped off, his head down. Here was a guy, a veteran of all that football, who obviously was hurt more than just physically. As he left the field, they gave him another ovation. I couldn't help feeling a deep sense of sorrow for him. And I had a lot of respect for the 49er fans who gave such a fine round of applause for a guy who was playing against them.

In Super Bowl IV I saw Joe Kapp as quarterback for the Minnesota Vikings fight desperately against the Kansas City Chiefs. It was a losing battle all the way because the Chiefs weren't about to drop that game. Joe was sacked late in the game and shaken up. He was a lonely looking figure that day in New Orleans as he walked off the field. The sun was going down, he had given it everything he had to give. As he moved slowly to the bench you could feel the last of his energy had been spent.

Later I came to know Joe better and respect him as a person when I worked on two movies with him, Semi-Tough and Two Minute Warning.

Hank Stram deserves a hell of a tribute for what he did in Super Bowl IV. Not only did he lead his team, the Kansas City Chiefs, to victory in the game, he allowed himself to be wired for sound. I don't think too many coaches would grant the public such a privilege. He probably thought it would be good for football, as it would give the fans an inside look at what goes on during a game among players, coaches and officials.

During the game the coach was upset because he felt we had missed a foul he had seen, and he started blasting, 'How could they do that? How could six officials do that? There's six of them out there and they missed it. Not one of them caught that!"

Tommy Kelleher, a top NFL official, was working on the Kansas City sidelines and heard Hank. As Tommy got closer to where Hank was standing, Hank walked out on the field and yelled something like, "Hey, Mr. Official, what's going on?"

Tommy was astute enough to know that there was no way he could possibly explain to a coach during the middle of a Super Bowl that someone could possibly have seen the play differently than he did. So, he just listened as Hank went on and on. Finally he turned his head a bit towards the coach and told him very congenially, "Hey, coach. You're on the field."

Immediately you heard Coach Stram say, "Oop," and he jumped back off the field. Tom had jarred the coach's mind enough to get him off the subject as well as off the field.

A few plays later though, there was a measurement right in front of Coach Stram. I remember this quite well. On the television you could hear the voices, but all you could see was a crowd of ball players.

The coach was saying, "We made it. We made it. We have a first down!"

And then another voice came in, mine, "Hold it, you haven't made it yet. Stretch out the chain." There was a kink in the chain and someone was standing on it. We pulled the chain out tight and they had made it by about two inches. "Now you've made it." I told everyone.

"That's great! What a great job of officiating. How about those guys. Aren't they doing a great job out there." So Hank sounded good through most of the game. The final score was 23—7, so he looked good too.

I have been asked many times if I have ever been involved in a protested game. The only "sort of" protested game I was associated with was between the Kansas City Chiefs and San Diego Chargers. The reason I call it a "sort of" protest is that I've never heard of a protest being upheld in pro ball.

The game was about eight minutes old when a TV time-out was taken and San Diego Coach Sid Giliman called me to the sidelines. When I went over to him, he told me, "That player, number 65 on Kansas City, is illegal. He doesn't have a contract on file in the league office."

I said, "I'll check it out," and ran across the field to Kansas City coach, Hank Stram, and asked him if that were true.

He said, "No, that's not right. We sent in his contract Friday, and the confirming telegram, too. That makes him eligible."

I ran back across to the San Diego side and told Coach Gillman. He replied, "Go tell him we're playing the game under protest."

So I ran back across and told Hank that Sid was playing under protest. He said, "Go tell him where he can stick his protest."

I replied, "That message you can deliver yourself, Hank. I'm getting tired of running back and forth across this field. What the hell do you think this is, Western Union? I'm going to start up this game again so I can get some rest."

To this day I never heard any more about the protest. I think the three of us were the only people who knew about it.

*Question. What was your biggest thrill as an official?*
*Answer. Super Bowl IV .*

## SUPER BOWL IV

"You've got the big one," Bob Baur, my field judge, called from Ohio to tell me during the Christmas holidays of 1969.

"Who told you? How do you know?" I asked. "They haven't contacted me about it."

"I just found out. Congratulations!"

"Now don't start kidding around about something like this."

"I am not. You're the referee for the Super Bowl. Don't tell me you're the last one to find out about it?"

"Listen. A few years ago a couple of guys started calling some other officials and told them they had the Super Bowl when they didn't. The guys told them that they weren't chosen for the playoff games because they were being saved for the big one. And it was damn cruel when they found out they didn't get it."

Bob told me who was on the crew and said, "I am not kidding you. Good luck." One of the men mentioned was Bill Schleibaum who lived in the Los Angeles area. I called him and he said he hadn't heard anything either. In a couple of hours the Western Union office phoned with the news. They read it to me and said they would have it delivered but I said, "No thanks. I am coming to get it myself." The big Christmas gift had come and the whole family started jumping around like a bunch of little kids in a pregame huddle. I was assigned Super Bowl IV, in New Orleans.

The crew was a mix of AFL and NFL officials. From the AFL there was me as the referee, Harry Kessel, the head linesman, and Charlie Musser, field judge. From the NFL there was Lou Palazzi, umpire, Bill

Schleibaum, line judge, and Tom Kelleher, back judge. Bob Finley of the AFL and Fred Silva of the NFL were the alternate officials. I wrote to all of them and asked them to be ready to talk to the rest of us about their positions and how they liked to work. The game would be the last time two true NFL and AFL teams played against each other for the world championship. The following year everyone would be under one banner, the NFL.

The pregame meeting with the people from CBS was so detailed and involved with what they wanted the officials to do, that I thought that I was going to be paid a talent fee from the network for working the game instead of as an official from the league. The pregame meeting on Saturday, with just the officials, had a lot of tension until I deliberately started calling everyone by someone else's name. When the supervisor of personnel, Mark Duncan, came in, I introduced him as if no one knew who he was. Everyone started to laugh and the pregame adrenalin was lowered.

He was joined by Mel Hein, the Supervisor of Officials for the AFL, and Art McNally, Supervisor of Officials for the NFL. They talked about the two teams in the game, each from their respective leagues. Mark and Art spoke of the overall play of the Minnesota Vikings, insights into their style of play, plays they might run, ways they might line up and what we could expect when they were in certain formations. Mel did the same thing about the Kansas City Chiefs. Nothing was mentioned about specific players.

I talked about how I wanted the chain brought in and how I liked fouls reported to me. I wanted them reported by color and number. Some referees like to have the other officials report to them by stating whether it's the offense or defense, and the number of the player, but what I wanted to hear was something on the order of HOLDING on 58, BLUE.

The commissioner's office felt there would be a lot of noise on Bourbon Street the night before the game, so we were assigned rooms on the top floor and at the back of the hotel, out of the way of the partying. The pregame celebration in the city was so wild that my wife and I decided to find a more quiet and unspontaneous setting— a movie, "Hello, Dolly."

When I awoke it was raining hard. I wondered later why I didn't get depressed thinking about how the game I had waited twenty-five years to officiate would be played against the elements more than the teams against each other. As I looked outside I thought about how I would have to watch the finest athletes in the country slide, fall and stumble with the ball popping and slipping to and away from them. We were told the day before that the field was covered, but that didn't matter now. There would be no tarp on top of the grass keeping the water out.

Because the parking facilities were sparse around the stadium Art McNally drove us to the ball game. I learned later that the Kansas City Chiefs' police escort didn't show up when the team wanted to leave their hotel for the stadium, so their bus left without them. They had to talk themselves through various security points along the way. (Imagine the Super Bowl as an intersquad game among the Minnesota Vikings? Sorry fans, but there will be no refunds.)

The first foul called in the game came when Minnesota punted to Kansas City early in the first quarter. The punter got the kick away, but when he did, four Chiefs were all over him. As I was walking off the penalty and getting ready to give the Vikings another first down, Hank Stram was telling his players what a stupid mistake like that had cost the team.

On my game report card where I recorded the fouls and offenders, I put down "Roughing the kicker front four, take your pick." You are allowed to touch the kicker if you hit the ball, but they missed it so they weren't allowed to come in there and level him like they did.

Tommy Kelleher, our back judge, came up to me after the play and said "Good call, John. That set the tone for the game."

For the most part he was right. When the kicker started off the field in the direction of the Kansas City bench I slipped up behind him and said, "Go to your left." He was probably looking at all four sides of the stadium at the same time. Thank God he didn't have to kick again soon.

Kansas City was a surprise team to make it to the Super Bowl for they had finished second in the AFL Western Division. But they beat favored New York 13-6 and Oakland 17-7 in the playoffs, and weren't favored to win this game either. Minnesota's record was very impressive They had lost only one game during the season, and beat the heavily talented Rams before coming to New Orleans.

I like Bud Grant's observation, "Defense wins football games. Offense sells tickets." He had the men to back up that statement in one of the most respected defensive lines in the game. Kansas City's defense was bent on keeping Joe Kapp from getting out of the pocket and using the ends for double teaming. It was a well fought contest up in the trenches, the front lines, however, the Chiefs' front line gave Dawson enough protection to work away from the oncoming "purple gang."

The turning point of the game, I felt, came when Kansas City scored to go ahead 16-0 in the second quarter. Kansas City had just kicked off after their third field goal and the Minnesota receiver couldn't keep control of the ball and lost it on a fumble to an offensive lineman. The ball was placed on the Minnesota nineteen-yard line. On the first play Dawson was dropped for an eight-yard loss. Wendell Hayes then blasted through the left side of the line for thirteen yards. A pass to Otis Taylor was good for ten yards and the Chiefs found themselves on the four-yard line, first down and goal to go. Mike Garrett lost a yard on the next play and then was held for no gain. With third and five the "65 toss power trap" play was called.

Hank Stram said, "It's a play we had for sometime, but we didn't use it until this situation. Our tackle (Jim Tyrer) pulled to influence his man (Alan Page). When Page came through he was open to the inside-out trap made by the right guard (Mo Moorman). It also took a good block by the tight end (Fred Arbanas) on the middle linebacker, and we got that."

Mike Garrett, who scored on the play, said later that, "It was the type of play that makes you look foolish if it doesn't work."

Garrett was so elated over making the touchdown that he rushed back through the pack toward the bench and ran smack into me as I was coming up to spot the ball for the extra point.

Both teams scored touchdowns in the third quarter but the game was out of reach for the Vikings. Minnesota got one penalty in the fourth quarter that hurt their cause. It was a late hit on Len Dawson, the Chiefs' quarterback. Just as Len rolled over and looked up to say something about the foul, my flag was flying right under his nose. It was fifteen yards for roughing the passer. He said, "Well, all right" and got up and ran to the hash mark. I got the players up, picked up the ball and started marching off the penalty.

Later I found out that Len was under more pressure than just the game. He had taken a lot of verbal abuse and innuendo during the week prior to the game from the media, regarding an investigation made by the Department of Justice. It was about his "supposed" associations with an illegal gambler. It was all disproved.

I felt even sorrier for Minnesota quarterback Joe Kapp after his last play of the game. The Vikings' last chance to win had slipped away and Joe just sat there on the field amid the blood, the mud and the dejection, frustrated from the day's work.

The game wasn't a difficult one to work. The great teams don't get to the Super Bowl by committing a lot of foolish fouls during the season. They play the game like they're supposed to. It's a tremendous responsibility for officials in a game of this magnitude, but the job itself isn't really difficult. I only called two fouls all day.

There were no complaints from either coach afterward. In fact, during the game there was less than the usual amount of negative comment from the sidelines. The players played the game and let us run the game. There were few rule changes to adjust for the game. The AFL's two-point conversion rule was tossed out and the official time was kept by the scoreboard operator, not the back judge, as it was done in the NFL. Both offenses used their league's ball.

I don't know what the best play of the game was, but it might have happened before the game started. A football fanatic from California flew in for the game. When he got into the stadium and found he had forgotten his whiskey, he left to go to a liquor store. Another car was blocking him and when he went to push it out of the way himself, five guards grabbed him and put him in a lockup outside the stadium for the entire game. It turned out he had been trying to move the governor's limousine.

The Tuesday following the game I was at my Kiwanis Club meeting in Southern California, and was introduced by Ken Lloyd, the president, who said, "Here is a guy who directed a game that half of the population watched. He had more control over what went on last Sunday than anyone else in the country. We watched him more than we would have the President of the United States." They gave me a standing ovation.

About a month after the game, I was playing in a golf tournament in Palm Springs and my partner on the second day was comedian George Gobel. We got around to talking about the game and I told him I was paid fifteen hundred dollars for working it. He said I was grossly underpaid for running one of the biggest shows in the world; that I had more attention focused on me in those three hours than any other segment of television, and that I should have been paid forty or fifty thousand dollars, "at least." I asked him if he wanted to be my agent, but he said, "I work alone, I'm a monologist."

The game meant a lot more to me than the fee I received. It was the end of the AFL. I was proud to be the only man to start and finish the league working at the referee's position. I was there at the beginning and I was there for the final play when the league came to a successful end. All the old AFL teams are now in the American Conference of National Football League.

# Questions

*A day does not go by when someone doesn't call to ask me something about football. These are not calls in the middle of the night from irate coaches and fathers, in violent protest over unbearable and impossible officiating, just the questions that have gone on during my time as an ex NFL official.*

Question: Do officials have any kind of idea who is going to win a game or how close the game is going to be?

Answer: Officials, as a rule, usually have one stock answer for that kind of question. If I knew who was going to win I wouldn't be out there calling the fouls. I'd be at the betting window.

Question: What was the toughest game you ever officiated?

Answer: The New York Jets vs. the Kansas City Chiefs, on December 22, 1963. It was so cold that my lip froze to the whistle. I pulled the skin off when I pulled the whistle away from my first tweet. For the rest of the game my lip throbbed every time my heart beat.

Question: Over the years, how has football changed?

Answer: First of all, football is like society in how it has adapted to specialization. Increased specialization on the field has meant that players only work one position. A quarterback used to kick, pass and run. Now, some of them only pass or hand off. A lineman used to play both offense and defense. Now he plays either offense or defense. There are no longer general practitioners in football. Everyone has been relegated to one function. In some respects football is also like a war. A war that has been brought down to scale so that the people can watch the teams fight over real estate. In the tenth or eleventh century it began as a kicking contest. A bladder of a pig or cow was kicked between two towns. Young and not-so-young guys would get out there and fight all day trying to kick it to the other town's steps. Somebody said that looks like fun to watch, but we can't be chasing them all over the countryside. Let's make it a game that we can sit and watch. And so there was soccer and rugby. America developed its "playing war" from them.

In American football you've got the guys up in the trenches, the men who play on the line. The guys involved in the individual fights. A lot of people come to games just to see them go at each other. They're the infantrymen. Each side has their tank troops that come in and

bulldoze over and capture real estate. The aerial corps plays up in the air in ballet dances, trying to come down with more land.

Each side has its own defense. The general staff is over on the sidelines with the general intelligentsia up in the stands calling down information to them. Spies are viewing the game for next week's wars. All of these elements are going on and the people watching the game are fascinated by the entire show.

Football and the hoopla connected with it seem to me to answer a need the American people have for a national ritual of semi-religious rite. Taken as a total, from the pregame ceremonies to the postgame ceremonies, everyone, players, coaches, cheerleaders, song leaders, musicians, the press, and the officials, act out their respective roles with great seriousness. It must be awesome to someone who sees it for the first time.

Question: Which sports have you refereed and are there any you wouldn't want to work?

Answer: Besides football, I have refereed basketball and umpired baseball on the high school and college level. I also refereed some Navy boxing shows during World War II. I would not care to work ice hockey because the players carry clubs, and the officials aren't allowed to. I think that's kind of unfair.

Question: What happens if the officials don't show?

Answer: The game isn't played. Players have got to be protected and that's one of the big reasons why we're there. I know of some high school games that were delayed because the officials were held up in traffic and I can't remember any of the teams wanting to go on and play the game without them. Ask any player at any level and he'll tell you there is no way he'd play without us.

Question: Don't you think if there are enough blatant mistakes by officials in a game that the game should be played over?

Answer: No. To my knowledge there has never been a game re-played. What one side would call a blatant error, the other side would say was a great call. I'd like someone to show me all the games, or even the one game that got ruined or lost, or whatever, by an official's mistake.

I've read about games in newspapers where someone on the team said that the penalties really cost us the game. Later in the article it mentioned the five turnovers and three missed field goal attempts, the four fumbles and seven interceptions, but not one wants to give those statistics as the possible reasons why the team lost. They want to believe, "The turning point in the game was when the officials called two straight penalties on us in the last quarter."

Well, the turning point for a team that thinks like that might be when they showed up at the stadium.

Question: Do you ever fear any kind of reprisals from fans you've left bereaved for calls you've made during a game?

Answer: No. I'd like to meet any bereft fans. Send them over and I'll explain that a football is a prolate spheroid eleven to eleven and a fourth inches long and it takes funny bounces.

Question: Have you ever been mistaken for a player and been tackled or found yourself in the middle of a pileup of players?

Answer: I haven't been mistaken for a player since I played at Stanford. Seriously, it's never happened to me. Interestingly enough, that's why officials wear plain knickers with no side stripes, like the players have. We wear striped stockings that are worn with the stirrups showing like baseball players. This is done so that a lineman or other player about to block or tackle will hopefully know that we aren't one of the boys.

Night Game Los Angeles Coliseum

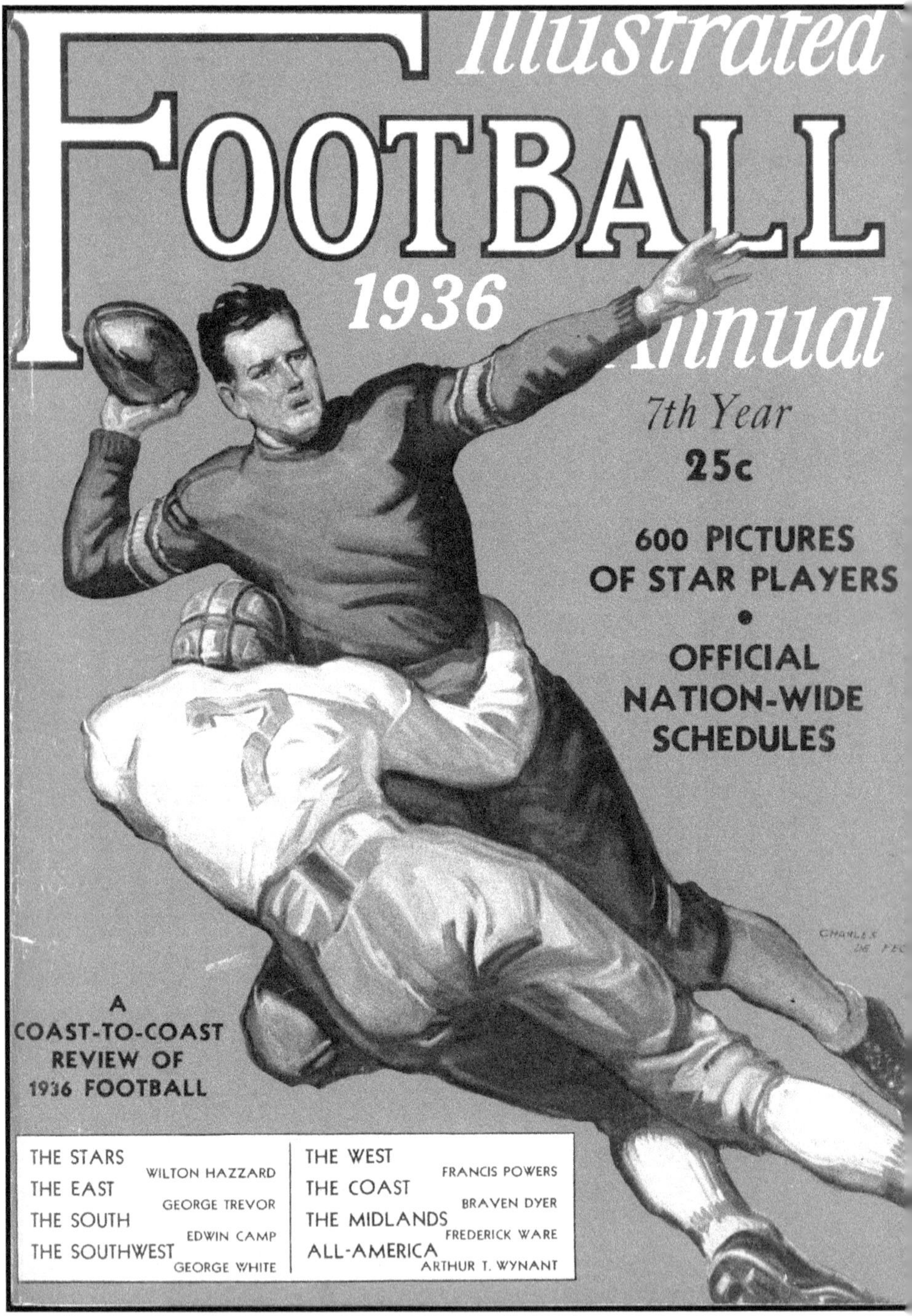


Football Illustrated, 1936 edition

# ANTITRUST IN PROFESSIONAL SPORTS:
# A VICTORY FOR THE PLAYERS

*The first lawsuit against the National Football League was brought by one of its players, Bill Radovich. This story is about the struggle for his rights within the system of professional football. It is complete with references to the laws it created and the workings of the legal system and attorneys who helped bring changes to the sport.*

The struggle for players' rights in the National Football League (NFL) did not begin at the time the National Football League Players' Association was created in 1956, or when it was formally recognized a few years later as a viable entity by the Commissioner of the NFL and its respective teams. The first assertive stance to defend players against the arbitrary powers of the league and owners came when Bill Radovich decided to sue the NFL for refusing to let him play in 1949.

Radovich was an All-Pro lineman for the NFL's Detroit Lions between 1938 and 1945. He had been one of the outstanding linemen in college at the University of Southern California from 1935 through 1937, receiving the honor of All-American. During World War II he served in the Navy and starred on the Great Lakes Naval Station Team.

Bill first learned of his rights as a player and the National Football League's reserve clause after his 1940 football season. He felt he was entitled to a $25 a game raise, instead of the $10 raise offered. After unsuccessfully renegotiating his contract by phone with Detroit Lions management, he sent the contract to the club, unsigned. When there was no response he returned to Detroit from Los Angeles to bargain there.

During one of the preseason practices the secretary of the team came out on the field and told him that they had not received a signed contract.

"I know, because I didn't sign it."

"Well, you have to or you can't play."

"What about the raise I asked for?"

"You're not getting it."

"Then I'll sign with the Redskins or the Bears."

"You can't. If you don't sign with us, we'll put you on the suspended list and no one will pick you up."

Bill signed with the Lions.

A few months after his successful 1945 season with the Lions, Bill contacted team owner Fred Mandel to try to arrange a trade so that he could be in California to care for his ailing father. Mr. Mandel would not accommodate him and Bill agreed to play for the Los Angeles Dons of the newly formed professional football league in the country, the All America Football Conference.

Before Bill signed his Dons contract he phoned Mr. Mandel to see if there was any room for negotiation. Mr. Mandel refused, telling him that he would not talk salary or any other element of the contract until he reported to Detroit. Mandel also warned him that if he did not sign with the Lions he would be blacklisted in the NFL, which meant he would be suspended from playing on any team in the League except the Lions for five years. Bill played two successful years with the Dons. He did not play the following year, 1948, because the team was making a youth movement and hiring only young players. Bill was thirty-three at the time.

At the end of the 1948 football season, Bill Howard, the coach and general manager of the San Francisco Clippers of the Pacific Coast League (PCL), offered Bill the opportunity to be a player coach. The Clippers and other teams in the Pacific Coast League had a close affiliation with the NFL. Howard did not know that the relationship between the two leagues meant that the PCL would abide by the suspensions issued by the NFL for players and thereby could not hire Radovich.

Before Bill could reply to the offer, Howard was notified by J. Rufus Kiawans, Commissioner of the PCL, that the offer would have to be rescinded.

The rule Radovich had broken was connected to the reserve clause as defined by the NFL members: a player who 'jumped' to another league could be kept from being reinstated to any of the NFL teams or their associate leagues until a five-year suspension period was served. Bill had been a victim of the arbitrary power of the reserve clause.

The NFL required all of its teams to use Uniform Player Contracts which at the time contained reserve clauses giving the teams perpetual rights to the services of their players.

Football was not the first sport to control the movement of its players. Professional baseball was invented with it. In 1879, less than twenty years after the declaration of the Emancipation Proclamation, organized baseball owners agreed that each could reserve a certain number of players which the other teams could not hire. When the National and American Leagues merged in the 1880's, a provision in their agreement gave each team the right to reserve a specific number of players. As Professor Lionel Sobel of Loyola Law School in Los Angeles, California notes, "Although the players' contracts made no mention of the teams' right to reserve them, the contracts did contain a clause by which the players agreed to be bound by all of the provisions of the National Agreement. Thus, the players were said to have assented to their reservation."

The arrangement was not acceptable to all players. In 1887 player representatives met with owners to attempt to dilute some of the power held over them. A new contract contained a reserve clause that stipulated that the salaries of each team's fourteen reserved players could not be reduced for the following season. Some of the players were still malcontent with the reserve standard and two years later created the first union of professional athletes, The National Brotherhood of Professional Players. One of the first orders of business was to demand that the reserve clause be eliminated. When the owners refused, the players formed their own league. The first judicial test for the reserve clause was when the major leagues sought to prevent players from jumping to the Players League.

Baseball won a major decision for its reserve clause in a landmark case in 1922 when it was challenged by the Federal Baseball League. The competing league contended that the National League's (the combination of the American and National Leagues) reserve clause and blacklisting threats to players made it impossible for the Federal League to hire quality players. The major leagues argued that it was not engaged in "trade or commerce" and that its activities were not conducted "among the states," and therefore it should be exempt from the Sherman Act and charges of monopolistic practices in bargaining for players.

The Supreme Court affirmed. "...Although the game made money it was not trade or commerce in the accepted use of the word," and as Judge Oliver Wendell Homes said, "Baseball is local in its beginning and its end."

At the time of Radovich's reserve clause discrimination action in 1948, the courts had recently reacted favorably to an athlete in the grips of the powers of management.

Danny Gardella, an outfielder with the New York Giants during the 1944 and 1945 seasons, played for a team in the Mexican League in 1946 When he returned to the United States he was suspended from playing on any major league team. He was one of eighteen who had played in another league.

Gardella sued the Commissioner, Albert "Happy" Chandler, and the New York Giants alleging that they had a monopoly on professiona baseball and that they had blacklisted him, which meant they were restraining trade and commerce in violation of the Sherman Act. He also demanded $100,000 in damages. In 1948 the judge at the District level agreed with organized baseball on the basis of the precedent of Federal Baseball v National League and dismissed the case.

The following February, Gardella won a momentous victory in the Court of Appeals. The Court reversed the dismissal, sending it back to the District Judge stating that a trial should be conducted to determine the veracity of Gardella's allegations. Judge Frank of the Appeals Court spoke of the case as being human emancipation from the reign of untested powers.

"...We have here a monopoly which in its effect on ball players like the plaintiff, possesses characteristics shockingly repugnant to moral principles that, at least since the War Between the States, have been basic in America, as shown by the Thirteenth Amendment to the Constitution, condemning 'involuntary servitude' .... For the 'Reserve Clause,' as has been observed, results in something resembling peonage of the baseball player .... The most extreme of these penalties is the blacklisting of the player so that no club in organized baseball will hire him. In effect, this clause prevents a player from ever playing with any team other than his original employer unless that employer consents ...."

"...The system created by 'organized baseball' in recent years presents the question of the establishment of a scheme by which the personal freedom, the right to contract for their labor wherever they will, of 10,000 skilled laborers, is placed under the dominion of a benevolent despotism through the operation of the monopoly established by the National Agreement."

The judge distinguished between Gardella and the Federal Baseball case of 1922. "In that earlier case, the court held that the traveling across state lines was but an incidental means of enabling games to be played locally .... Here the games themselves, because of radio and television, are, so to speak, played interstate as well."

The decision in favor of Gardella and the other suspended players prompted Gardella to seek reinstatement for the coming baseball season while he awaited trial. Though the preliminary injunctions for him to play were denied by the courts, Commissioner Chandler reinstated him and the other players.

Attempting to save face, Chandler acknowledged he had allowed the players back, and added, "But I would not do it until the court said

I did not have to." The Commissioner did more to keep the potential public defeat of baseball in the antitrust arena when it settled with Gardella without going to court.

The result of Gardella v Chandler was that organized baseball found itself defendant in eight federal antitrust lawsuits. Three bills were introduced in the House of Representatives and one in the Senate, all of which would have granted complete exemption to baseball from antitrust laws. After reviewing these cases, Congress was assured by baseball that the legality of the reserve clause would be tested in the future in court with the rule of reason. No legislation was enacted. Although the House Subcommittee on the Study of Monopoly Power did not approve legislation from the hearings, it did recognize the reality that "In the past the reserve clause has been employed as a 'war measure' to fight the development of competing leagues, sometimes to the expense of the individual players."

The Subcommittee was not in favor of unequivocal immunity for baseball from antitrust, but it did conclude that the sport had to have some form of reserve clause to operate successfully. Gardella gave impetus and hope to Radovich. "I didn't leave the country. I just played in another league." Although the settlement figure for Gardella was said to be much less than $100,000, Radovich set that amount as what he wanted as compensation for being denied the right to earn a living as a football player and coach.

A copyright attorney suggested to Bill that he meet with a very young and successful antitrust attorney, Joseph Alioto. After a few preliminary meetings with Alioto, Radovich decided on his own to write a letter to the Commissioner of Football, Bert Bell, explaining his desire to return to the Lions or any team that the league felt he should play for. Alioto was upset when he learned of the letter. "All the Commissioner has to do is send you a letter telling you to report to a team and then have you released from that team after the first day of practice and we have no case."

There was relief. Within a week Bell had responded, "If you want to come back and see me in my office in Philadelphia I will be here, but I will not promise you any reinstatement." Not only had the Lions refused him, now the Commissioner would not assure him of being placed on any team. Radovich's case had improved. The lawsuit was filed in July of 1949. Radovich charged the NFL, its teams and the Commissioner, the PCL and its commissioner, and the San Francisco Clippers with conspiring to monopolize professional football in the United States by destroying the All America Football Conference and by blacklisting him. After the complaint was filed, Radovich went to Canada to play for the Edmonton Eskimos. Near the end of the season in November, Alioto called him. The NFL attorneys in San Francisco had suggested a settlement sum and Joe wanted Bill to stop on his way back to Los Angeles to discuss the details. The legal firm representing the NFL told Alioto that $18,000 was all they could budget for a settlement, but that they would have to verify it with the Commissioner before it could be officially offered. Bell would not allow it. No settlement, nothing. The NFL then hired another attorney for the case, Marshall Leahy, who was counsel for the San Francisco 49ers, one of the three teams in the All America Football Conference who survived the collapse of the league and was granted status in the NFL.

The NFL was successful against Radovich at the lower Federal Court level. The case was dismissed by the court and the legal consensus was that the results of current cases relative to antitrust and sports would affect Radovich's appeal.

Three of the lawsuits which had prompted an attempt for immunity to antitrust for baseball were received by the United States Supreme Court and were decided together under the name of Toolson v New York Yankees in 1953.

George Toolson was a player with the New York Yankees farm system. In protest of his assignment to the Binghamton, New York team from Newark, New Jersey, he refused to report and was therefore placed on Binghamton's ineligible list, which barred him from participating in professional baseball.

He brought his case to the Appeals Court level where he received no relief. The court ruled that baseball was not subject to existing antitrust legislation.

The Supreme Court concurred so far as that decision determined that Congress had no intention of including the business of baseball within the scope of Federal antitrust laws.

Alioto's advice to Bill concerning the impact of the Toolson case was set forth in a letter from counsel Elwood S. Kendrick who wrote on April 12, 1954: "In view of the Supreme Court ruling in the baseball case, it is the opinion of both Mr. Alioto and myself that this case will be controlled by the baseball decision.

"We know of no difference in the facts that would make professional football an activity in interstate commerce when baseball is not." Radovich would not sign a dismissal of the case, however. An associate in Alioto's office, Maxwell Keith, noticed the refusal and decided to continue the struggle. He would write the legal brief and argue the appeal.

The Court of Appeals affirmed the lower court's decision to dismiss the case in September of 1954. Keith then filed a petition in Supreme Court to grant a hearing for reinstatement of the lawsuit in May of 1956. On October 8, Radovich was granted the right to be heard by the Supreme Court.

A few months later, in February of 1957, the case was reinstated by the Supreme Court: Radovich's case would be tried in the lower court. The Supreme Court declared that football is not exempt from antitrust as baseball is.

Keith summarized the decision more philosophically: "Radovich established that an individual injured by antitrust laws was entitled to recovery. You did not have to prove that the public was injured."

At this time not only was the NFL being pursued by its number one exiled player, but its masses, the players who represented its teams on the playing fields, were struggling for their rights also.

An organization called the National Football League Players Association was created in 1956 under the guidance of Cleveland attorney

Creighton Miller. "We don't consider ourselves a union. We don't like to call ourselves a union," Miller declared as he and a representative group of players united to demand personal dignities from the owners of the League. The players wanted improvement in their economic condition with some control over their destiny.

Norm Van Brocklin, the leader of the players in the formative stages of the association, stated, "It is the contention of the Players Association, and this is the basis of the organization, that all teams should offer equal minimum benefits, that benevolent paternalism, as practiced by some of the clubs is fine, but that it should be standardized throughout the League."

Some of the concerns of the players were over preseason training, payment for exhibition games, the recognition of the Association by the League and a minimum salary for players.

Commissioner Bell had countered with a suggestion that a player representative for each club take the players' grievances to the team owner and if a settlement could not be resolved at that level then the representative could go to Bell who would be the final arbiter.

The players wanted recognition and Bell promised them he would seek it at the annual league meeting in January of 1957. The only thing the meeting accomplished for the players was a declaration from Bell that the League would not deal with any bargaining agent for the players.

Several bills were introduced in Congress to exempt football and other sports along with baseball from the antitrust laws. At one hearing Bell testified that the players did not need antitrust protection. The National Football League Players Association received its first official public recognition when Congressman Emanuel Celler asked Bell if he had in fact recognized the NFL Players Association. Bell replied he had.

A formal acceptance of recognition did not come from the League, though in December it yielded to players' demands for a minimum salary, payment for preseason games, medical expenses and payment in case of injury.

While Radovich was giving advice to Van Brocklin on how success-fully to approach the Commissioner, Keith was preparing for trial. In January of 1958 he received a call from the NFL office that the League wanted to settle without going to court. In April they agreed on the amount of $42,500.

Radovich was not happy with the amount. "If I had known it was taxable I would have demanded we go to trial. That amount could not make up for the loss I had to take without playing or coaching. I never had a full career in football and nothing could compensate me for that. At least not $42,500."

"But I was relieved, too. I felt like a piece of furniture pushed from one room to another for the eight years I fought this. I was drained physically and emotionally. I was alone most of the time, actually alien-ated from pro ball. The players who were on my side couldn't come out and say it for fear of their own position. They were working for the people I was trying to beat."

The settlement came in April of 1958, at the beginning of baseball season. "Perfect timing for football to bow out without any public notice. The news hit the eighth or ninth page of every big city paper if it was mentioned at all. Not many knew that the NFL had bought their way out. And damn cheaply, too," concluded Bill.

In retrospect, there were players who were granted reinstatement to the League after having played in other football leagues. In the case of Bernard J. Mertes, for instance, the Commissioner, on September 7, 1949, allowed him to return.

In a letter to Mertes, the Commissioner enthused, "You are a Free Agent and may sign with any team in the National Football League who may desire your services and with whom you may come to an amicable agreement as to contract."

Mertes played for an NFL team owner who was not as adamant about retaining him as Mandel was about Radovich. But, if Mandel had released Radovich from the imposed suspension of the Commissioner, the case, <u>Radovich vs the NFL</u>, would not have been filed. And we would not have had a case which created a practical way to bring the power of the owners under judicial review, a case which gave the players momentum in their struggle for rights and dignity. Sports had taken a further step in solidifying the forces of its greatest one team, the players.

Stanley Silver, Artist

# Soccer

*The first game ever played is now a sport that covers the entire world. Here is the story of its origins, complete with terms and descriptions of the game.*

## The History Of The Game—the Very First Game

Although there is no conclusive evidence to connect today's game of soccer with ancient ball games, there are very interesting similarities between the games of the different ages.

Kemari, the ancient Japanese football game, was played as early as 600 B.C. Descriptions of the game show goals made of five-yard high bamboo stakes. Like its predecessor, the Chinese game of Tsu Chu, which has been traced to 3000 B.C., Kemari had both religious and political significance. The balls of these early games were leather skinned, stuffed with animal hair, or animal bladders filled with air.

An Athenian gravestone dating approximately 2000 B. C. depicts a man juggling a ball on his thigh. Although the Greek game Episkyros did not include kicking, its purpose was for two teams competing against each other to advance a ball up and down a field in an attempt to get it past a goal line.

History is replete with other types of ball games with features indigenous to football. Tribes of the Philippine Archipelago, the Maoris and various Polynesian peoples played with oranges and coconuts as well and used both their hands and feet. In Mexico and Central America during the pre-Columbian period, ball games were an important segment of religious life for both the Azetc and Toltec civilizations. The Eskimo game of Aqsaqtuk is a form of soccer, played on ice or snow. The balls are filled with moss, grass, caribou hair and sand. Traces of soccer elements were evident in the early ball games played in Celtic England. Though the ball was not kicked, the athletic purpose of the games was to 'project' a ball into a goal. It is believed that when the Anglo-Saxons conquered England they inherited various Celtic games.

Another theory of origin of today's game is that the Normans brought it with them to the British Isles in the 11th century. It was a wild game with arenas being the vast spaces between villages. Teams consisted of a multitude of players who ran and kicked the ball through open fields and city streets. Such popular games were called Mellays from which the word melee is derived. The game brought out an unruly athletic chaos which caused successive bans by royalty, the first of which was by Edward II in 1314.

The sprawling game continued in various forms until it was organized at the school and college level at the beginning of the 19th century. Each school developed its own rules dependent on the playing space available. In 1823, a student at the Rugby School could not withstand the restrictions of using his 'feet only', and picked up the ball during the game and began running with it. Thus marked the beginning of rugby. The history of both these sports paralleled each other in their early formative days. The Football Association was established in England in 1896. In less than a decade, the 'other' sport had its Rugby Union.

### The Players And Their Positions

CENTER FORWARD
Because of his position on the field the center forward is usually the highest scoring member of the team. In general the center forward stays in the midfield line area when his team is on defense. He is the point person in offense but is not excluded from playing defense when needed.

INSIDE FORWARD
The inside forward has two primary tasks, that of developing and completing or finishing attacks on an opponent's goal. He also controls the midfield area. On defense the forward provides ready outlets for clearances out of his own defense in the beginning stages of a counter attack. When the inside forward comes to defense around the goal area he is responsible for defensive corner kicks.

OUTSIDE FORWARD
The outsides (wings) run by the sidelines on their respective sides of the field. Each wing has one man (fullback) covering him. His main respon-

sibility is to get free from his fullback so he can receive passes from his teammates.

## HALFBACKS
Halfbacks are also known as midfielders. They have a dual responsibility, both defensively and offensively. Games are won and lost in the midfield. Good midfielders are good defenders but they are needed more for their creative skills. They are the 'brains' of the team, as they create plays for the forwards to finish.

## FULLBACK
The fullback's primary playing purpose is to defend against the opposing wings or outside forwards. His position is in the area between the wing and the goal, trying to keep the outside forward from moving into the area. Fullbacks play in tandem positions. If one challenges the forward on his side, the other fullback goes into the middle of the field across the goal to guard against passes.

## GOALKEEPER
The goalkeeper guards the goal area more closely than any other player. He plays in the goal and penalty area. When he has made a save, the final stoppage of an offensive threat, he has full control of the ball in beginning a new offensive attack. He is the only player to use his hands, and only within the penalty area.

Olympic Soccer

# Soccer Terms

ADVANTAGE RULE:  Applied by the referee when in his judgment penalizing an infraction would give an advantage to the offending team. He signals that play is to continue, and no penalty is called.

BOOTS:  The traditional name for soccer shoes.

CATENACCIO:  A defensively oriented system of play incorporating tight, man to man marking of opponents and providing for a free man called a sweeper, or libero, who stands behind the last line of defense and covers every teammate in the defensive third of the field.

CAUTION:  A disciplinary action taken by the referee signaled with a yellow card and officially recorded against a player guilty of misconduct a second offense warrants ejection from the game (red card).

CENTER CIRCLE:  The circle at the center of the field, drawn with a radius of 10 yards from the center spot.

CENTER SPOT:  The point in the center circle (the midpoint of the halfway line) from which kickoffs are taken.

CHARGING:  Use of the shoulder to charge the shoulder of an attacking player in order to dispossess him of the ball. It is the only time deliberate body contactis allowed in soccer.

CHECKING RUN:  A feinting technique that involves taking a few quick steps in one direction before turning and sprinting in another.

CLEARING: Throwing (by the goalkeeper only), kicking, or heading the ball high and wide to move it out of the goal area or the penalty area.

COLLECTING:  The technique of receiving a ground or air ball, then bringing it under control before putting it into play.

COMBINATION PASSES:  A series of short, low passes used by 2 or more players to maintain possession of the ball while they move toward the opponent's goal. Also called "combination play."

CORNER KICK: A direct free kick taken from a corner area by a member of the attacking team if the ball goes out of bounds across the goal line and was last touched by a member of the defending team.

COVER: A defensive concept that involves taking a goal side position to support, or back up, a teammate who is challenging an opponent for the ball.

CURVING PASS: Kicking the ball to the right or left of center to send it in the opposite direction. It is also called the "bending pass" or "banana pass."

DRIBBLING: Dribbling is the art of moving the ball on the ground in a series of short pushing kicks. It is the best way to overpass an opponent. Players dribble to move into a position where they can pass the ball to a teammate, or shoot at the goal.

Here is a list of MUSTS for the dribbler:

1.  The dribble is to be a part of your natural running style so as not to slow your movements.

2.  The ball is kept close to you to assure possession.

3.  Keep yourself well balanced so you can move in any direction at any time.

4.  Do not look at the ball, instead watch your defenders and look for players to whom you can pass the ball.

There are three ways to dribble: with the inside, outside and instep of the foot. For inside the foot dribbling contact the ball midway between the big toe and the heel or at the large joint behind the big toe. Strike the ball sending it in a path to be hit or nudged at the same place on the other foot. For the outside of the foot dribbling only one foot moves the ball. That foot is turned in slightly with the toes pointed downward. The ball should never be more than one or two feet ahead of the dribbling foot. While dribbling from the instep position point your toes downward.

To keep the ball on the ground as you move it your foot should be raised at least two or three inches when pushing it. You can help this to happen by crouching over the ball. If you lean backwards as you move the ball the tendency is for your foot to hit under the ball causing it to lift away and go out of control. The mastering of dribbling requires you to feel that the ball is an extension of your foot. A 'part' of your body. You want to dribble whenever you can, wherever you go. You don't carry the ball to practice, you dribble it there. No matter what the surfaces are, whether it is asphalt, dirt, rock, or grass, they all offer you practice for improving your ability to react to changes in speed and direction. You want to establish a rhythm and a harmony between yourself and the ball. You want a soft touch, one that gives you the confidence that you are in control of the ball.

When dribbling to beat a defender always keep the ball close to your feet, don't chase it. For deception, dribble slowly and straight toward him watching his hips to see which way he is leaning. Suddenly lean to one side or drop your shoulder and as soon as he makes a move, move the ball the other way and dribble on past him. After you have beaten him look for a teammate to pass it. You don't want to give him a chance to come after you and you don't want to dribble just for the sake of dribbling. You will be more effective passing the ball instead of dribbling it over long distances. Try to keep yourself between your opponent and the ball. You will want to do this shielding especially when he charges you or tries to go around you to get to the ball. Caution!! If he gets rough in his attempt to get the ball by playing you instead of it, don't fight back. Let the referee take him out of the play.

DEAD SPACE: For the attacking team, areas of the field occupied by players of the opposing team.

DIVING: A method used by the goalkeeper to stop or deflect low and medium high balls aimed at the goal.

DIVING PIT:  A surface of foam rubber or sawdust used to absorb impact when a goalkeeper or other player practices diving saves, diving headers, or scissors kicks.

DROP BALL:  A ball dropped by the referee between 2 players, 1 from each team, to restart the game after he has purposely stopped play for a no penalty situation. The ball is dropped at the spot where it was last in play unless this happens to be in the penalty area, in which case it is dropped at the nearest point outside the penalty area. A goal may be scored directly from a drop ball kick.

FIRST TIME:  Passing the ball, either by kicking or heading, passing without stopping it first.

FREE KICK: A placekick awarded to a team when a player of the opposing team is penalized. A free kick is either a direct kick, called for a serious offense, or an indirect kick, called for a minor infraction. Players on the offending team must remain 10 yards away from the ball until it is put into play, unless they are on their own goal line between the goalposts.

GHOST DRILL: Practicing soccer skills with no opposition other than the goalkeeper.

HANDBALLING: A major violation, the intentional use of the hands other than by a goalkeeper. The penalty is a direct free kick.

HEADING:  Using the forehead, between the eyebrows and the hairline, to propel and direct the ball.

INDIRECT FREE KICK:  A free kick that cannot score a goal without the ball first being touched by a player other than the kicker. Also a specific penalty called for minor infractions.

JOCKEYING:  A maneuver in which a tight guarding defender gives ground, leading the player in possession of the ball into a less dangerous area of the field. It is also called "shepherding."

LINESMEN: The 2 officials who assist the referee. The linesmen patrol the touchlines and carry flags to signal the referee when a ball has gone out of bounds, there is an offside, or a foul has been committed that the referee might not have seen.

LIVE SPACE: Open, or free, space created for a teammate by enticing an opponent away from an area.

MARKING: Guarding an opponent.

NEAR POST: The goalpost closest to the ball.

OBSTRUCTION: Deliberately impeding the progress of an opponent instead of playing the ball. The penalty is an indirect free kick.

ONE POUCH: Passing or shooting on goal without stopping the ball first; that is, on the first touch.

PENALTY ARC: An arc drawn outside the penalty area at a radius of 10 yards from the penalty spot. No players are allowed within this arc when a penalty kick is being taken.

PITCH: The traditional name for the soccer field.

PLACEKICK: A kick taken when the ball has been placed in a stationary position for starting the game and for restart situations.

POKE TACKLE: Use of the toe to poke the ball away from the person in possession. The poke tackle can be executed from the side or the rear of the opponent.

PUNCHING: A means of saving a goal or deflecting a ball by hitting it with the fists. Can only be used by the goalkeeper and he must be in the penalty area.

SQUARE PASS: A pass made laterally to a waiting or moving teammate across the field.

SWEEPER:  Often the last player, except for the goalkeeper, on defense. His main responsibility is to prevent attacks on goal. Also called a "libero."

TARGET PLAYER:  Usually the central striker, who is tall and especially skilled in receiving air balls.

THROW IN:  The method of putting the ball back into play after it has gone out of bounds over the touchline. A member of the team opposing the team that last touched the ball must throw it onto the field from over his head, using both hands and keeping a part of each foot on the ground either behind or on the touchline. The ball is thrown in from the point where it went out of bounds. A goal cannot be scored directly from a throw in.

TOTAL SOCCER:  A system of play involving constant changes of players' positions as the teams gain and lose possession of the ball. Also called "positionless soccer."

TOUCHLINES:  The boundary lines at each side of the field. If a ball goes completely over the touchline, play is stopped and restarted by a throw in from the place where it went out of bounds. Also called "sidelines."

VOLLEY KICK:  A kick taken before the ball touches the ground.

WALL:  A human barrier of at least 3 players, used to aid the goalkeeper in defending against free kicks when they are specifically so awarded. Players may line up 10 or more yards from the ball to form a barrier between the kicker and the goal.

WEAK SIDE:  Pertaining to the side of the field away from the ball.

The Olympic Flame

# THE TORCH: FROM ANCIENT GREEK FESTIVAL

## TO MODERN OLYMPIC DRAMA

*The first Olympic Games of the Modern Era in America were in Los Angeles in 1932. It was the 10th Olympiad of this era, and 10th Street in Los Angeles was named for it, Olympic Boulevard.*

*The First Olympic Torch Relay was in 1936 in Berlin. The first American Olympic Torch Relay was for the 1984 Los Angeles Olympic Games.*

*I was fortunate to have been on the staff of the 1984 Olympic Organizing Committee, and to have travelled with the Torch Relay on some of its path from New York to Los Angeles. Here is a brief view of that journey.*

The ancient Greeks had torch races to honor their gods. The carrying of the flame to a sacred altar was once only a cultural rite. To preserve the purity and power of the fire it had to be moved with speed. Hence developed competitions to see which individual or group relay could move the torch the swiftest. The winner of the event known as Lampdedromia (from the word lampas meaning torch) was given the honor of lighting the fire in the name of the patron deity of the city or the god in whose honor a festival was being held.

People of all ages participated. The races were on foot or horseback, with as many as 48 members on a team. The distances ranged from 800 to 2,500 meters (approximately 1½ miles). Runners competed wearing only leather or metallic crowns with flame shaped pieces of bone or wood setting on them. The races were usually held at night and captured a special fascination for the Athenians, as depicted by Plato in "The Republic."

Baron Pierre de Coubertin, founder of the modern Olympic Games, felt the Olympic tradition must have ceremony. "...The question of the 'ceremonies' is one of the most important to settle. It is primarily through the ceremonies that the Olympiad must distinguish itself from a mere series of world championships. ...People met at Olympia to make both a pilgrimage to the past and a gesture of faith in the future. This would be equally fitting for the restored Olympiads. It is their function and their lot to unite across the fleeting hour the things that were and the things which are to be. They are preeminently the festivals of youth, beauty, and strength. In this keynote we must seek the secret of ceremonies to be adopted."

The Modern Olympic Games have incorporated the torch and torch relay as one of its ritual ceremonies. The Olympic hymn was created for the first Olympiad celebration in 1896. The awards stand was introduced at the 1912 Games in Stockholm. An official Olympic flag was unveiled two years later at the twentieth anniversary of the founding of the International Olympic Committee. The Olympic Oath became part of the traditions at the 1928 Amsterdam Olympics, along with a flame which was lit and burned throughout the duration of the competitions. A torch was lit to open the festivities in 1932. but it was not until the following Olympiad in Berlin that the historic dimension of a torch relay was unveiled.

Dr. Carl Diem, a former runner and Chef-de-mission for the German Olympic team of four previous Olympic Games, was inspired to create a torch relay ceremony from a model portrayed in the writings of Plutarch. An all weather magnesium torch weighing 1½ pounds and 2¼ feet in length was developed. A special concave reflector was made to focus the sun's rays and create fire. A sacred grove in Olympia, Greece was designated as the starting point of the torch relay.

The lighting of the Olympic Flame is very sacred to Olympic tradition. As the opening addresses are being made in Olympia, a procession of priestesses is formed which moves toward the altar of Hera, where, with the help of the concave mirror, the Head Priestess lights the Olympic torch from the sun's rays. Carrying a branch from the olive trees of the sacred altis, the procession enters the Ancient Stadium. The Priestesses then encircle the altar, the Prayer to Zeus is made and the Head Priestess lights the torch. She then gives it to the first torch runner who turns and runs to the Coubertin Grove. When he arrives he lights the

Olympic altar, raises the torch in tribute to Baron Pierre de Coubertin, then runs in the direction of Athens.

The torch, its symbol and hope in the Olympic tradition is best epitomized by the Head Priestess of several Olympiads: "I have never been able to free myself from the feeling that I am coming into contact with something majestic and beautiful, created not just by a human fantasy but by a deep longing for principles of reason, for a festival of the humane ideas. The Flame which is kindled in ancient Olympia carries a message of peace, confidence and hope to all people on this planet."

The first relay began on July 20, 1936 for the Berlin Olympic Games when fifteen Greek maidens walked in unison through the tunnel passage leading to the remains of the ancient stadium at Olympia. They placed the large, concave reflector on one of the marble slabs which marked the starting line for sprinters of the ancient Olympic Games. The reflector focused the rays of the sun on a torch held by one of the women.

When the torch was lit, she carried it to the altar by a sacred grove of trees and ignited a brazier there. A young Greek runner dipped his torch to the brazier and then began the first leg of the 12 day, 3,000 kilometer journey to Berlin. The torch was carried to Athens, then through Bulgaria, Yugoslavia, Hungary, Austria and Czechoslovakia on its way. Fritz Schilgen, a former athlete, ran the last leg of the relay down a series of steps and onto the stadium floor to the resounding music of Beethoven's Ninth Symphony.

The relay was an overwhelming success and was destined to become an Olympic fixture. The 1948 London Games' torch relay began during a Greek civil war. The first runner was Corporal Dimitrelis of the Greek Army. He appeared fully dressed in his uniform. He laid down his gun, changed into running attire and began his run.

The torch was carried through eight war-torn countries of Europe. The last leg was run in Wembley Stadium by British middle distance runner John Mark, president of the Cambridge University Athletic Club.

For the Helsinki Olympiad of 1952 the flame went airborne for the first time. It was flown from Athens to Copenhagen, Denmark, then transported by ferry to southern Sweden. A relay of runners, bicyclists and motorcyclists brought it to the stadium where Olympic champions Paavo Nurmi and Hannes Kolehmainen were the last two runners.

In 1956, after the flame was flown from Athens to Darwin, then Cairns, Australia, it was carried to Melbourne. Ron Clarke, the National Junior distance record holder at the time, and future Olympian, lit the fire in the stadium. Four years later the naval sailing ship Amerigo Vespucci took the flame to Italy where Giancarlo Peris ran the flame on its final lap in Rome.

The Tokyo Olympic torch relay distinguished itself from all others by its all-encompassing flight routes. The airplane carrying the torch stopped in eleven countries on the way to Japan. In each country a mini torch relay took place from the airport into the capital city and back to the airport. It then toured the Japanese islands before Yoshinori Sakai, a Japanese boy born in Hiroshima the day the city was destroyed in World War II, ran in the stadium with the dramatic flame for the final distance. The history of Christopher Columbus was the focus of Mexico City's torch relay for the 1968 Olympics. The torch went to Columbus' birthplace in Genoa, Italy; to Barcelona, Spain, the port at which he was received by Queen Isabella after his initial voyage; then to the port of Palos where he departed to the New World; and finally to San Salvador, the exact site of his landing. Eduardo Moreno became the first athlete to carry the Olympic torch over water when he swam with it to the shore from the ship that docked in Vera Cruz, Mexico. The Mexico City Games was also the first time a woman ran the final leg. Enriqueta Basilio, twenty, a Mexican National record holder, ran the torch into the stadium and up a long stairway to light the Olympic flame.

The Munich torch relay of 1972 followed in the same footsteps as the 1936 Berlin run. The flame was escorted by four great Olympic track athletes on the last segment of its journey into the stadium. An interesting added feature was the flame being taken to the Olympic venues at Kiel, Kassel and Augsburg. A special relay of twelve motorcyclists carried the flame to Nuremberg. In 1976 Montreal was quite innovative with the use of modern technology. When the torch reached

Athens it was touched to a sensor which coded the energy of the flame and beamed it to a satellite. The satellite then transmitted the signal to Ottawa where it ignited a torch. Then off to Montreal. The descendants of the founding peoples of Canada, Sandra Henderson of Toronto and Stephane Prefontaine of Montreal, both fifteen, carried the flame into the stadium together.

The Moscow Games of 1980 had a Torch Relay of Champions. Bulgarian two-time Olympic champion Boyan Radev received it at the Greek Bulgarian border. Olympic champion Iordanka Khristova of Bulgaria passed the torch over the Bulgarian Romanian border to Romanian Olympic champion Dimitru Pyrvulesku. At the Romanian Soviet boundary Olympic champion Nicolai Martinescu of Romania handed it to Soviet Olympic champion Pytor Bolotnikov.

Sergei Belov, a member of three Soviet Olympic basketball teams, carried the torch on its final leg into Lenin Stadium. A moment before his run, giant telescreens in the stadium flashed pictures of Soviet cosmonauts circling the earth. Belov then circled the track and ran up a ramp of shields held up over the heads of Red Army soldiers to the top of the stadium to light the flame.

It was just as spectacular as Rafer Johnson running the final part of the 1984 Los Angeles Olympic torch relay, with a moving ladder raising him to the top of the Los Angeles Memorial Coliseum to light the Olympic rings.

The story that follows is of the people who were among the millions who loved and cheered the Olympic torch as it swept through hearts of Americans welcoming the world to the XXIII Olympiad.

"Few ceremonies in the Olympic Games are more suspenseful than the arrival of the Olympic flame in the stadium during the opening ceremony. As the last runner in a long relay across continents and oceans carries the torch into the stadium, the impact on athletes and spectators alike is tremendous. The crowd falls silent in the seconds prior to the appearance of the last runner, only to erupt in a whirlwind of sound as the runner finally appears."
—Andrew Strenk, Ph.D. Olympic Historian and Olympian, member of 1968 USA Olympic Swimming Team

# THE LOS ANGELES OLYMPIC ORGANIZING COMMITTEE HAS AN IDEA

In the initial planning for the 1984 Olympic Games, the Los Angeles Olympic Organizing Committee envisioned a torch relay that would pass through each of the 50 states and capitols and the District of Columbia. And all within an 84-day period. The concept of a Youth Legacy Kilometer (YLK) program was first discussed at a planning meeting in March of 1981. The YLK idea was a means of raising monies to support existing youth activities.

American Telephone and Telegraph (AT&T) was designated an "Official Sponsor of the 1984 Olympic Games" and "Official Sponsor of the Torch Relay Run" on June of 1982. By January of the following year AT&T had created a torch route. Two months later the Torch Relay Foundation was incorporated for the purpose of education and charity within the guidelines of the Internal Revenue Code. Each $3,000 donation for participation in the torch relay could be tax deductible by individuals and corporations.

Three groups were initially granted the right to solicit the general public to participate in the relay: Girls Club of America (July 12, 1983), Boys Club of America (July 13, 1983) and YMCA (July 18, 1983). The Special Olympics became the final organization to qualify for the fund raisings in January of 1984. Funds raised from the YLKs would be divided between the parent organization and the local level club.

It was agreed that the LAOOC would be responsible for overseeing the fund raising aspect of the torch relay, and that AT&T would supervise the logistics. In May of 1983 the LAOOC hired Joel Fishman as Vice President for Torch Relay Operations.

Exactly one year before the opening of the 1984 Games, July 28, 1983, the torch relay kilometer program was announced in a press conference in New York City.

"We want part of the legacy of the 1984 Olympic Games to be a lasting commitment to the youth of America," LAOOC President Ueberroth said. "We believe that local organizations, as well as individuals, businesses and other groups, will join hands to help relay the Olympic Torch across the country. They'll share in the excitement of the relay and help to open the Olympic Games and they'll be sowing the seeds for youth athletic programs that will give youngsters opportunities to play and enjoy Olympic sports for years after the Games."

The LAOOC did not actively sell the kilometers, but released information to the general public regarding the opportunity to participate in this historical event. Linda Lucks, the manager of public relations for the torch relay, said, "There was virtually no advertising or marketing budget. We sent public service announcements and slide presentations to television and radio stations who could mention the torch and the telephone number where people could call to get more information. We received free advertisement from various magazines. Task forces were set up in major metropolitan areas. Civic and business leaders and representatives from Olympic sponsors including Buick, Anheuser Busch, First Interstate Bank, Converse and United Airlines, joined forces in helping us spread the word.

"The kilometers were difficult to sell in the beginning because we could not guarantee people exactly where they would be running."

An example of the corporate involvement was at Pacific Bell which was instrumental in reaching its goal of selling 1,000 kilometers.

The Southern California Youth Legacy Support Committee was formed under the leadership of Gerald D. Foster, Pacific Telesis Group Region Vice President. The idea for such a committee was formulated by Jim King of Pac Bell, Lilly Lee and Gilbert Vasquez. Helping them to formulate plans in the San Diego area were Art Madrid, Director of Governmental Relations for Pacific Telephone. Wilma Steinhauser was responsible for the task of coordinating all planning with business, legal, entertainment, medical and civic leaders.

One of the business and civic leaders contacted by the Pac Tel group was Carl Karcher of Carl's Junior restaurants. Karcher contacted 100 friends and associates to attend a meeting. He began the session by telling them that "By just showing up you have become part of my committee to become involved in the Torch Relay."

The response was a resounding success. One of the people in the room at the South Coast Plaza Hotel in Costa Mesa was Michael Reagan, son of President Reagan. Michael did not have to be convinced of the idea, for he had already purchased a kilometer.

"I should have bought another one," said Reagan, "but I didn't realize that until I was running with it. I didn't want to give it up."

On September 14, 1983, Turner Industries, Inc. was named "Manufacturer of the Olympic Torch," becoming an official supplier of the 1984 Olympic Games. In January of 1984, a 15-member advance team, hired by the LAOOC, began a detailing process for making the route workable. Among the numerous variables to consider were highway safety, designating possible locations for celebration ceremonies, the selection of streets that would accommodate the most spectators, and contact with law enforcement agencies, local government officials and AT&T Pioneer personnel.

After assembling this information, a trial run of the relay was set for a distance of 800 miles along a part of the actual route. This run-through helped in the timing of the relay, procedures for the changing of vehicles and staff, and modifications of the torch.

By March the advance staff began determining how many YLKs could be run in a day, and where they would be run. Meeting places for YLK participants were set where they could pick up their Levi's running uniforms and Converse running shoes. As the May 8 deadline approached, relay staff members also contacted runners to find out about their medical history. During this time Pioneer staff members were obtaining permits in cities, contacting local officials and finding overnight stop points where the parade of vehicles could park.

Though the trial run helped establish scheduling guidelines, there were unforeseen contingencies that needed spontaneous and creative reactions to control during the run. Detours were made to accommodate recent road construction projects. When an air conditioning unit was installed atop the EMS (Emergency Medical Services) vehicle on a stopover during the run, clearance for underpasses went from 13 to 14 feet. Because of weight limits on bridges some vehicles would have to go around a city or town and meet the caravan on the open road.

Timing was challenged by weather and the size of the crowds. The torch itself was a lightning rod. In a lightning storm in Lansing, Michigan the torch was stopped for forty minutes. Extra thick and exuberant crowds made some locations an hour or longer to traverse instead of the planned ten minutes.

For reasons of security and not wanting to constantly update changes in the daily routes, the detailed list of the streets where the torch would be carried was given to the press only on the day before it arrived. This policy was changed for California to dilute the clusters of crowds. "We wanted to spread out the crowds as much as we could. To do that we gave the press the route plan a week in advance. This gave people a chance to go to one of several places instead of converging on one spot," said deputy press secretary for the torch, Lindsay Chaney. In Los Angeles, as in other Southern California areas, was the phenomenon of the 'follow,' where people would drive or run to several locations along the route. It was a chase, a hunt, an attempt to see the torch in as many places as possible.

The torch was welcomed everywhere, but in some places there was concern. The safety engineer, the captain of the Highway Patrol and the governor of one state said no initially to the torch traveling through. They claimed it would be too dangerous due to the summer and heavy truck traffic. Officials of the towns bordering the main road, however, overwhelmingly guaranteed police patrolling support. "Everyone rallied around it," says Jeff Black, torch team advance person. "In some areas we were promised two or three officers and when we got there there were ten or twelve. Everyone wanted to be part of it."

The Director of the Torch Relay Project and Associate Vice President of the Torch Relay Foundation, Joel Fishman, reflected on the impact of the relay on the country. "It was big then, when it happened, and almost bigger than life later. Yet it was real, very real, and very special to all of us. The country was overflowing with pride. It was a great equalizer, uniting everyone of the host nation."

And, though many people had a responsibility in making it successful, Fishman's decision to hire Wally McQuire to be field consultant and logistical manager of the relay was considered to be one of the most important steps. "Wally made it all work. We also have to look at the wonderful partnership between the private and public sectors. The torch relay served as a strong model for future relationships between these areas."

# THE TORCH FAMILIES

Leona Weinberger lived next door to Oscar Pattiz in Los Angeles in 1932. Oscar was a young, successful attorney who thought he knew the answers to everything but how to show more interest in Leona. The Olympic Games was a perfect idea. He worked on the Coliseum staff and shyly suggested to her that she come to Opening Ceremonies.

She said yes, and yes again and again to a standing invitation for every day of the two weeks of the Games that summer. The rest is part of the book of personal Olympic history. They were married two years later.

Oscar died in 1979, a few years after the Los Angeles Olympic Organizing Committee was formed to administer the XXIII Olympiad of 1984. When the torch relay was announced, the family wanted to enter as a symbol of the full circle of their lives together. Carrying the torch would be a grand celebration of its unity and connection to its Olympic roots.

There are five Pattiz children: Eve, Jackie, Cathy, Happy and Nancy. All of them were represented in the six consecutive kilometers which were run in honor of Oscar and Leona.

The plans were furthered by the renting of a bus and film crew to go to the family's kilometers in Oxnard, sixty miles northwest of Los Angeles. As the family members completed their kilometer they ran ahead and stood on top of their bus that was moving in the torch caravan. For three miles after their runs there were six runners with six torches, leaping and jumping, reaching the torch higher and higher.

Leona Pattiz was diagnosed in 1982 as having cancer, and was given no longer than six months to live. She held on longer. One of the keys she credited to her survival was the spirit she had from her children and grandchildren taking part in the Olympics. She lived long enough to prove it: long enough to see films of her family's runs, long enough to see the torch carried past her bedroom window in Los Angeles, and long enough to see the Olympic Games held in Los Angeles for the second time. A perfect ending. Leona passed away three days after the Games.

There was other family sentiment in the Los Angeles area connected to the relay. The sons of Ginny Hirsch ran at one-thirty in the morning and were awarded the key to the city of Canoga Park at that time. Ginny worked as a volunteer at the UCLA Village during the Games. A professor at UCLA ran with his son.

The family of David Roberts gave him a torch kilometer as a symbol of his wellness on Thanksgiving of 1983. It was a recuperative hurrah, a hope for continued good health. David is President of the Pritikin Longevity Center.

Nat Handel sponsored his children's running with the torch and was a supporter of the LAOOC's Patron's Program which enabled numerous senior citizens, physically challenged and disadvantaged youth to attend the Games at no personal cost. "Not only did the torch give some extra warm feelings to our family, it inspired my children, Jon, Nanci and Richard, to become more runners than before."

The plans of Colin Gilbert included four generations. He wanted his father, child and grandchild to run, and was ready to support such a venture of pride but it was not logistically possible. Instead he had to 'settle' for doing it alone, with one consolation, however. "I ran right by the place where I grew up. It was like I was carrying a light for the kids who were down on the beach that night chasing grunion fish on the sand as I had done many years ago."

Brad Sawtelle passed away on a Monday. His son Greg's tenth birthday was that Tuesday.

One of the many sensitive things Peter V. Ueberroth did as President of the LAOOC was make sure Greg ran a torch kilometer in honor of his father. Brad was one of the prime creative people involved with the publicity of the torch relay and other LAOOC related events.

Greg spent the summer of 1984 with his grandmother in Twin Falls, Idaho. The torch passed through that city and Greg had one of the proudest moments of his life running with it.

"It was scary though the night before whenever I thought about how I might fall with it. I knew I didn't have to worry because there would be a runner with me, but still it was a little scary."

Greg's mother, Lee, summed up the family feeling: "The Organizing Committee showed sincere emotional support for our family with the way they cared for Greg."

The Olympic torch touched many a dramatic family memory. Jon Tokunaga ran in Tulelake, close to the Oregon border, by the Japanese relocation camp where his mother was taken during World War II. His mother was there to witness his run. Lennart Andersson carried the torch during the 1952 Olympic torch relay in the Helsinki procession. His wife, Britt, approached Del Taco Corporation of Costa Mesa, California to support a kilometer for Lennart to run in 1984. Not only did they sponsor him, but their son Ken as well. Young men and women from Japan were sponsored by Sister Cities International to help promote mutual understanding throughout some of California's 50 sister cities.

Al Stewart, an 85-year old retired fireman, competed against twelve other convalescent home participants, in and around Sacramento in the special event called the Olympiatrics. Al won seven competitions including the racing wheelchairs and won the honor of carrying the torch. Peter B. Smith of Sacramento lost 150 pounds when challenged by a local firm which said if he could lose the weight they would put him in the relay. Peter not only won his way to a kilometer, he also helped generate over $25,000 for the Special Olympics program in the city.

The YMCAs and Olympic Torch Project of Sacramento were very imaginative in accommodating community residents who had been assigned to distant places to run in the relay. Camps were set up at Adin and Susanville in the far northern section of California. Private pilots were available to fly those individuals who needed transportation.

A special event was staged at the state capitol when the torch arrived on July 15. Local residents who ran in faraway towns wore their uniforms and participated in a run around the capitol building so that their friends and families could see and photograph them carrying the torch. There was also a post relay appreciation reception. That coupled with an invitation by Governor George Deukmejian to meet with the torch bearers in his office gave extra honor to the festivities.

The most touching moment came when Billy Mills, the 1964 Tokyo Olympics 10,000 meters champion, ran with the torch at the state capitol and handed it to twelve-year-old DannyHansen. Danny has muscular dystrophy and is a member of a family which includes two Eagle Scouts and one Junior Olympic Gymnastics Champion.

## THE SOUTH—KNOXVILLE TO ATLANTA

A few blocks south of the University of Tennessee in Knoxville, three young men leaned against a Volkswagen van parked on a dirt lot across from a railroad overpass. On a turnabout island in the street which ran underneath the railroad bridge stood the next runner, a champion Tennessee high school distance runner, awaiting the torch.

"How long before it gets here?" one of the young men asked.

"I don't know. It's supposed to be here at 6:10," another said.

"What time is it now?" the third man asked.

"About 5:45."

"I hope it's late. Let 'em take their time. I love to see everyone coming out of everywhere. Gives me a chance to see who's still around."

The crews from local television stations were setting up their equipment. The mother of the runner walked across the street to give him a blanket. A young boy rode his bicycle back and forth repeating, "It's not here yet. It's not here yet."

"You want to come with us?" one of the men asked the third. "We're going to follow it for a couple of hours. I want to see it when it gets dark."

"Sounds good. Why don't we follow it clear cross the country?"

"Take a couple of months off work, that'd be great."

"When you come back just tell the company you were vacationing watching the torch and listening to everybody yell and scream. How could anyone fire you for that?"

The other man, a truck driver, said, "Can you imagine how'd it be for me to go cross country with my rig with everyone waving flags everywhere I went?"

An older man leaned outside the screen door of the bar next to the lot and asked everyone, "When's it coming? How long will it be before it gets here?"

"Any minute now," someone answered.

Within a few minutes the boy on the bicycle turned the corner by the bar and gathered speed as he rode and called out, "It's here! It's here!"

The flame was exchanged and the runner set out with a slow methodical stride passing under the railroad bridge. A few blocks later he reached the University of Tennessee campus.

Students were gathered along the streets of the campus. The crowd swept along as if a wind following the runner, closing the road behind him and the caravan as he moved. From the air the crowd looked like a hand that had grabbed the runner, while another hand opened to let the next runner fly out. In a fast and poignant moment Honey Alexander, the wife of the Governor of Tennessee, took the flame from the high school runner and ran off campus.

The torch went on to Gatlinburg that evening where it stopped. The following day was the Great Smokey Mountains, a few of the towns of North Carolina and Georgia, and a very special visit with Steve Streater.

Sports play an integral part in the life of Steve Streater. He was a star football player at Sylva Webster High School in Sylva, North Carolina and an All Atlantic Coast Conference player as a defensive back and punter at the University of North Carolina in Chapel Hill.

On April 30, 1981 Streater signed a contract in Washington, D.C. to play for the Washington Redskins of the National Football League. He then flew to the Raleigh Durham airport. While driving his car home it spun out of control and hit an embankment. Steve's neck was broken causing a severe paralysis.

Three years and one month later, Steve Streater was a carrier of the Olympic torch. He held it high as he steered his electric wheelchair into the downtown area of Bryson City, a short distance from his family's home in Sylva. Walking with him on his journey were his sister, father, mother and Uncle Ray. His best friend sat on the rear bumper of the photographer's flatbed truck, clapping and cheering for him. As he entered the city there was a giant roar. "It was the most outstanding moment of my life. Holding the torch I was touching the whole world, and bringing everyone together. I've accomplished a lot in my life, but this is the most important thing I have ever done. Why the accident happened I'll never know, but if it hadn't I might not have been carrying the torch. This is more important than football."

His days in football are not over. Steve is the coach of a local semi professional team and a state coordinator of public services programs for North Carolina.

"It's not what you do with your body that makes you great," an on-looker said. "Steve is one of the greatest football players from this area. But today he showed more human courage and dignity and was more of an inspiration to us all than whatever he could have done playing in the pros."

While Steve acknowledged the cheers from his friends and neighbors, approximately 30 miles away in Andrews, North Carolina, Teresa Hensley stood outside the Lee clothing manufacturing company awaiting the torch. "I won't be in Los Angeles for the Olympics so the torch is as close as I'll ever be to the Games. And my friend and I aren't going back to work until we see it."

A few weeks before the torch entered Georgia, Skip Miller, an AT&T engineer, spoke to the Sandy Springs Chamber of Commerce. He gave the members of the chamber an idea of what to expect when the torch arrived.

"Imagine it's May 31, late on Thursday afternoon. The streets are lined with people. In the distance a light appears in a long moving caravan. The excitement mounts. The crowd cheers. Children are perched atop their fathers' shoulders to get a better view. The torch is moving down Roswell Road through Sandy Springs business district as it heads toward downtown Atlanta on its way to Birmingham, Alabama.

"You and I and our children will actually have a chance to participate in Olympic history right here at home." Nancy Nix, aged nine, of Gainesville, Georgia, was one of those children. She announced to her mother one morning at breakfast that she was going to be an Olympic torch runner. There was only one obstacle as far as Nancy was concerned; the rules stated that runners had to be at least ten years of age.

Mrs. Nix presented her case to the proper authorities and the age requirement was altered. "From then on we baked Easter cakes,

Mother's Day cakes, pound cakes and sheet cakes. Nancy made craft jewelry which she also sold."

While Nancy ran her kilometer Mrs. Nix ran alongside the road carrying a thick photo album with pictures of every cake and every piece of jewelry she made and sold. Mr. Nix was on the opposite side of the road taking pictures.

One of the torch staff vans stopped to pick up Mrs. Nix as she ran. Instead of running out of breath trying to keep up with Nancy's pace, Mrs. Nix nearly did explaining the pictures.

At the morning torch celebration in Dahlonega, Georgia, held at six o'clock, bands played and balloons waved.

"We spend more money getting ready for this than we do on our own elections," a local resident said.

"I am glad we didn't have to decide between this and spending it on an election. You know what would win," another offered.

On its way towards Atlanta the torch stopped at a home near Cummin where elderly people sat outside dressed for its arrival. Georgia State Police posed for pictures with the people and the torch. An entire school in Cummin waited outside on the grass for the torch while a doctor's office changed its hours until evening so the doctor and staff could take in the waiting excitement. A teacher at another school, who was besieged by parent permission slips to release children for the torch, wanted to know, "When is someone going to come to take me out of school so I can watch?"

A farmer stood on a roadway and focused his camera but the torch was carried too quickly for him. He fell as the torch passed and called out, "You're going too fast. Come on back here." A father and son whiled the waiting time away throwing a baseball to each other at the family's pharmacy in anticipation of the man's daughter running by with the torch.

As the procession passed a radio station near Cummin, two employees ran to greet it carrying a large American flag. A security person with the relay called out: "Do you want us to take it with us? We'll get it to Los Angeles."

The two looked at each other puzzledly about the possibility, then one said, "All the way to Los Angeles?"

"Right to the stadium for the Opening Ceremonies."

They both jumped and ran across the street to hand the flag to him.

If you were in Atlanta the night the torch came through, you were given four hours of continuous international entertainment presented by AT&T, Colony Square, WSB 99FM and Coca-Cola USA. More than 20,000 people packed the Colony Square area to witness performing arts members from the following groups: The Academy of Indian Dance and Music, Pegasus Greek Dancers, Hebrew Academy Chorale, The Young Americans, The Buffalo Chips, Choral Guild of America, African Dance Ensemble, Izvorni Eastern European Folk Dancers, Northside School of the Arts, and the Spirit of Atlanta Drum and Bugle Corps.

The exchange of the torch in Colony Square was filled with spectacular excitement. Brian Dyson, the president of Coca-Cola, handed off to Anrewayne Thunder Sun Forsythe.

"It is a significant statement of support for the Olympics and the torch relay to have the president of one of the major corporate sponsors of the Games running with the torch. The spirit has definitely caught everyone," said John Bevilaqua, Vice President and Director of Public Relations for the LAOOC.

Andrewayne Thunder Sun has many talents. He is an artist and plays three musical instruments. He is also a natural runner and at the age of twelve represented his family of seven.

For three months prior to the relay Andrewayne trained with his older brother and coach, Aric, sixteen. They worked together using a baseball bat to simulate the torch.

"I wanted Andrewayne to run as a way of enhancing his self-image," said his father Peter. Alisabethe and Peter Forsythe are the parents of five adopted Indian children and are closely involved with the International Children's Institute which sponsored his kilometer.

The crowd at the torch exchange between Mr. Dyson and Andrewayne was tightly packed along the streets and sidewalks of Colony Square as the nine o'clock torch time approached. Andrewayne held his seven-year-old sister Anja to help ease his overwhelming anticipation. High-intensity lights beat down on him, police motorcycles patrolled the area keeping the pass-off area clear, as people moved to get their best possible position to watch.

When the flickering lights of the caravan came into view the crowd held their arms outstretched and roared. Andrewayne looked ahead to see the running space he had. His body shook for warmth and in excitement. As Mr. Dyson approached, the people with cameras in the crowd and the photographers in the press truck took aim and flashed their lights to match the fireworks that sprayed across the sky. Andrewayne had enough energy "to fly. And I didn't have to run fast at all. I practiced to run fast but there were so many people and so much excitement I thought I would never get there."

But he did. He flew right into the arms of his brother who was standing at the end of his run waiting to share the excitement with him.

Olympic torch lady lighting up the world.

# COLORADO SPRINGS

There was a symphony orchestra and three hundred members of the USOC Training Center among the 15,000 spectators on the field and in the stands at Colorado Springs' Garry Berry Stadium to welcome the torch. The stadium was built to hold 4,000 people.

Jenny Storms, the national slalom champion for twelve-year-old skiers, ran the torch into the stadium. She told Lou Ann Varikowa, the torch advance coordinator, "This is my first Olympic event." First of the many she has considered. The symphony played the Olympic theme as she entered. When she exchanged the flame with Otis Forest, the orchestra played the Battle Hymn of the Republic. Otis then ran out on a ramp over the heads of the crowd to the theme of America the Beautiful.

The skies had threatened to rain all day. The clouds were ominous gray, dark blue, grayer and darker blue. "But you had to wonder," said Dick Sargent of the LAOOC, "if there wasn't some kind of natural magic involved because as soon as the athletes were introduced and asked to stand, the sun dropped down from beneath the clouds and shone right on them.

"To relieve some of the tension I had from anticipating to talk to everyone, actually to keep myself from getting all choked up on my words, I began taking pictures of the crowd as I reached the podium. They laughed and I was able to talk without any breakups."

Sargent, one of the major executives of the LAOOC, headed the overall operations directly responsible for the torch relay. He had the honor of accepting the sacred flame in Greece for its flight to the United States and traveled with the torch in other various locations along the way.

"Among the many high points I had during the torch run was seeing a man on a grassy knoll off the road in New Jersey play God Bless America with a trumpet. And, anyone who wasn't on the steps of the Philadelphia Museum of Art, where the movie Rocky was filmed, when a blind runner ran up them with the torch certainly missed an exceptionally powerful moment." Sargent ran with the torch in Parker, Colorado. "My concern was the altitude: how I was going to run at 6,000 feet, but when I got hold of the torch I had so much adrenalin running through me I wasn't thinking about anything else but carrying it. I had so much energy left when I finished I ran right back to the beginning to get my things. A few youngsters ran with me and I let them carry the torch. They'll have that moment to remember forever. I'll never forget the horse and rider who paralleled me alongside as I ran with the flame."

When Dick returned from one of his trips on the route to the Olympic Organizing Committee, he talked to the working staff at a general meeting. He never completed the story about the man who played God Bless America. The words got blocked in his throat and there wasn't a dry eye in the room. "From all the people I have spoken to, who carried the torch, the experience ranked right up there with getting married and having their first child."

## AMY AND DANNY

Twenty-one minutes. Go ahead, see how long it takes you to run or walk or wheel yourself through the distance of a kilometer. If you do it in less time than twenty-one minutes, you have done it faster than Amy Haas of Mission, Kansas.

Amy is eight years old and has cerebral palsy. She ran with the torch in her hometown. Every step she took her knees buckled. Every step she took she could have collapsed. Every step she took the torch relay people and security support staff were ready to help. Every step no one was needed. She did it all alone.

There was an aura of silence that surrounded each step of her way that erupted into joyous triumphant cheers as she moved past. It was as though the silence was there to steady her; as though the crowd was witnessing one of the greatest victories of courage; and touched in this special way rejoiced in loud and vibrant cheer.

Mark Zangrando, a torch advance person, said it was definitely the most moving of all personal stories. "We saw so many moving personal experiences I think we could have become jaded, but this was the most moving of all."

One of the biggest surprises for the torch caravan people was the crowd in Salt Lake City. Thirty thousand were expected to greet the torch. Over a quarter of a million lined the streets along the 13-mile route through the city. The run was culminated by the dramatic run of Special Olympian Danny Searles who ran to meet the mayor of the city at the state capitol. The crowd chanted, "Danny, Danny, Danny," as he carried the torch. At the exchange the mayor hugged him and ran the flame to the capitol building, the crowd shouting the initials 'U-S-A, U-S-A!"

## WASHINGTON CHEERS THE TORCH WITH THE FOURTH

The Torch celebrated the Fourth of July throughout the amber hills and fertile farmlands of eastern Washington. Runners carried the flame from Mesa to Cashmere, through the towns of Othello, Moses Lake, Ephrata, Quincy and Wenatchee.

Ken Hendrix, sixty-two, who has been a marathon runner more than half of his life, ran through Moses Lake sponsored by the Telephone Pioneers. As he dedicated his torch to the Pioneers, he created a most beautiful visual metaphor. "I figure the torch is a needle, and that the runners carrying it were a thread sewing our nation up again."

Husband and wife, David and Linda Robinson of Coeur d'Alene, Idaho, also ran in Moses Lake. After their run David exclaimed, "It's the only way I can take part in the Olympics."

The Los Angeles Olympic Organizing Committee has included youth in the making of Olympic history with the establishment of programs that involved them in the learning and participating in Olympic sports before and after the Games. Three of the thousands of children who participated in these programs flew to the Washington area with Olympian Wayne Collett to run that day.

"Kids and small towns are what this is all about. I can hardly watch films of the relay without getting torn up by the effect it has on the people," Collett said after running a kilometer in Ephrata. "I can't tell who is more excited, the people or me.

"In Moscow (for the 1980 Games) they took the kids out of the city to make way for the tourists. In Los Angeles we have programs to help kids get to events who could not afford to go on their own.

"For me running with the torch was more exciting than running in the Games and winning any medal. In my Olympic race I felt, 'I am finally here. I have worked eight years to get here. It was sort of anticlimactic after looking forward to it so long. With the torch I had no idea how excited I would be. I literally jumped two feet into the air when I saw it coming towards me.

"Seeing the flame touched off a feeling of pride deep inside me. You can be proud of your country during the Olympics because of the athletes who are representing you; wanting them to do well because they are from your country... but the torch brings out your pride in your own country."

The psychic energy for Wayne was not totally spent during his kilometer. "When I finished I took off by myself and ran for at least five miles along a river. And I had not run for five years. I had so much pumped adrenalin inside me, that I had to go out and run it off. I needed to be by myself to appreciate the completion of the moment, one of the most important in my life. If I had a choice of competing again or running in a torch relay, I would want to carry the torch. I just hope the Games come back to America again, and in my lifetime.

"But most important of all is what the youth programs sponsored through the Organizing Committee have done. And, here were some of those children running in one of the biggest spectacles in American history. That was very gratifying to me. It was a winning spirit for everyone. The torch transcended everything."

Three youths with Collett: Cruz Fino, Rebecca Quintero and Keith Nathaniel of Southern California, ran their kilometers at the Fourth of July night celebration at Wenatchee's Apple Bowl stadium, the site of the annual Apple Blossom Festival.

"I was kind of scared," said Fino, thirteen. "I'd never really stood in front of that many people before as the center of attention." Fino and the other two had just witnessed a fireworks display of a red torch spitting fire, bordered by an American flag and Olympic rings lighting the dark stadium.

Having the torch and the Fourth at the same time gave a special spirit to the people of Wenatchee.

Mayor Jim Lynch enthused, "Everybody was cranked up for it. This is the first time I had people calling me to volunteer to help. I had to turn down offers."

There was more than the Olympic torch that concerned Americans that day. On the east coast the Statue of Liberty torch was being taken down for restoration.

One of the bystanders watching the relay pass commented, "This torch relay is like the spirit of that lady touching everyone in America."

That spirit moved on to Cashmere from the 3,000 people in the Apple Bowl and the many thousands outside who gathered in great cheer. When it arrived the crowd that came to greet it had a hushed moment and then began singing God Bless America.

## AN ALMOST TWENTY-FOUR-HOUR DAY

Each torch day was planned for seven hours of down time, when the flame, the torches and its accompanying crew were at rest. It was not always like that. The day the torch took over San Francisco, Oakland and the rest of the northern peninsula on its way to San Jose was almost a twenty-four-hour day.

The torch team assembled at 4:45 AM near Hamilton Air Force Base in Marin, just north of San Francisco. Forty-five minutes later the relay continued. Three bridges had to be crossed and each with time restraints. The torch had to be on the Golden Gate by 9 AM, crossing over the Oakland Bay Bridge between 1 and 3 in the afternoon and on the San Mateo Bridge by 7 and 9 at night.

Mayor Dianne Feinstein welcomed the torch on the San Francisco side of the Golden Gate at 10 AM, proclaiming it Olympic Torch Day for the city. In Golden Gate Park senior citizen Edna Karatics was helped around in her wheelchair with the torch by California Boys Club's Boy of the Year. At the Army Presidio a battalion of troops ran behind an officer, dressed in T-shirts, fatigues and boots. The torch went through the business and Fisherman's Wharf districts, the streets packed with spectators, and all while the city was welcoming the Democratic National Convention.

But there was enough time for Mayor Wilson to make a speech at a luncheon at the convention, then helicopter across the bay to Oakland to be on hand at 3 PM to receive the torch in his city. Chikako Nakashima of Fukuoka, Japan was flown to Oakland for the torch run for a presentation with the mayor as part of the Sister City program. The torch, of course, was there, having reached the Oakland Bay Bridge by 1:50 and off it by 2:30.

Transamerica had given California Governor Deukmejian, and Mayors Feinstein and Wilson, kilometers to run or designate someone to run for them.

After a trip through the east San Francisco Bay region, the torch crossed the San Mateo Bridge between 7 and 8 PM. and arrived at Stanford University by 11. "The crowds on campus were so thick we had to push them out of the way for us to make it through," said Mavis Segal, a member of the advance team.

And, finally to rest in San Jose, thirty miles south of the university at 2:30 AM.

## AND WHEELS TURNED FOR THE TORCH

For the first time in Olympic history wheelchair races appeared in 1984. The determination to include these competitions came from people like Jennifer Smith who met early on with the LAOOC and other organized athletic groups to have the physically handicapped recognized internationally through athletic performance.

Smith, the 29-year old model, nurse and paraplegic, was one of the final torchbearers in Los Angeles, sharing the torch-carrying activity with Dr. Paul Berns, president of the National Spinal Cord Injury Association, California Chapter, which sponsored Jennifer.

"Traveling side by side, this is a celebration of the integration, finally, of wheelchair sports with able-bodied sports in the Olympics," Jennifer stated.

Since January of 1983, Jennifer trained for what she hoped would be an Olympic marathon for the physically challenged. She spent most of that time working out in Ohio exercising and testing in the futuristic laboratories of a doctor who is experimenting with paralysis patients. To further complicate a hopeful walking recovery and her intense training schedule, were bouts with a broken leg and pneumonia. Setbacks she has come to regard as routine in her quest to walk again.

Wes Piotrowski, Jennifer's father, watched in proud admiration as torch onlookers described her courageous will. "She calls it courage, but we used to call it 'stubbornness.'"

After she finished her kilometer she breathed a sigh of satisfaction. "It was exhilarating. You know how things that are exhilarating are sometimes exhausting even when they're not? I mean there was so much energy coming from all those people that one short kilometer seemed like forever."

Although Jennifer Smith was not able to compete for a place in the Olympic women's race for the physically challenged, she was there at the beginning of a new chapter to Olympic history, the establishment of two races for men and women who compete naturally on wheels.

On the same day Jennifer wheeled her way with the torch, one of the oldest living Olympians achieved another mark in Olympic history.

The captain of the 1924 USA Olympic rugby team was Alan Williams. The woman who tied for the 80-meter hurdles championship of the 1932 Los Angeles Olympic Games was Evelyne Hall Adams. They were together as one moving entity in the Olympic torch relay.

Mr. Williams was ninety-two years old. Mrs. Adams was seventy-five. He is confined to a wheelchair. Mrs. Adams is an active Jazzerciser and cyclist. On a street in Marina del Rey, near the main offices of the LAOOC, Evelyne pushed Alan along for their combined kilometer.

Talk about history and the honor. They were the only two Olympians who participated at the same time in the relay. Both have also served as past presidents of the Southern California Olympians. She was also an active member of the 1984 Olympic Spirit Team.

Mrs. Adams' Olympic history goes back to 1927 when she collected money to send the USA Olympic team to the 1928 Games in Amsterdam. "I have been a pioneer volunteer for the Olympics. And nothing was more gratifying for me than when we received the torch to carry. It is impossible to articulate in words the pride I had when the extensive glow of the torch was passed to me. Just the heat from the torch itself gave me a surge of pride and patriotism. Being part of the Games as a competitor and then running in the relay is beyond what anyone can really express."

Evelyne was upset with one thing about the torch. She couldn't take it home with her. The nursing home that sponsored her wanted to keep it for their own nostalgic display.

What has helped to keep Evelyne in good physical health is her participation in the Jazzercise fitness programs. Judi Sheppard Missett, the founder of Jazzercise, and 275 of her franchise system associates and instructors were among the many who donated their dancing talents to the Opening Ceremonies of the 1984 Olympics, coming from as far as Sweden, Italy, Japan and Germany.

In making the Olympic torch relay part of her way of giving back to the community from which she had made her professional beginnings, Judi's kilometer contribution was donated to the Carlsbad Boys and Girls Club, the place she began getting phone call inquiries about her fitness techniques in the 1970s.

## THE TALE OF THREE CADRE RUNNERS

When John Dunn, an AT&T private line switchboard coordinator, decided to be a cadre (long distance) runner, he did it with the thought that it would be a lonely trip through desolate areas with occasional sparse crowds. He was flown from Los Angeles to Salem, Oregon to begin his week of running from Gladstone, Oregon.

"At the orientation meeting held when we arrived we were told that crowds would treat us like movie stars. People would ask us for autographs and a lot would be made of us just because we were bringing the torch through. I listened but did not realize how much I would have to discipline myself to separate myself from what the crowd was really celebrating, the torch. The celebrity business is for the torch. It's not me. But the feeling of carrying it was unbelievable.

"I went from an unknown runner to a much cheered unnamed hero, and back to a completely unknown and unrecognized ex torch carrier within one week."

John did not even have to run in the beginning. "The crowds were so thick I had to walk. The first leg of my running was through a tunnel. There it was, a flickering torch in the dark, and when I came to the end of the tunnel a solid rock cliff was on my left and a river to my right.

It was totally magical. And there I was, like a moving line that separated the river from the mountain."

Whenever John became overwhelmed with how important he had become, he began thinking of the honor it was for him to run in the same section of the run as Olympic decathlon champion Bob Mathias, and marathon great Bill Rogers. "My real importance came from helping a seven-year-old boy keep the torch up while he ran and tried to get himself in front of his father who was taking pictures."

The warmth of the people along the way will always be remembered. "The city of Adin, California doesn't have more than 500 people, yet I'll bet there were close to 5,000 people out waiting to welcome us and help us dance ourselves silly the rest of the night. The atmosphere was always jubilant everywhere we went."

John suffered the same 'post relay partum' that others felt when they returned home. The symptoms were deep withdrawal. "Why not? No one was watching whenever I ran. No one even came out to cheer."

Phil Torres ran on the same cadre team with John. A special relationship developed between Phil and the people in the Corvallis, Oregon and surrounding areas. They followed him from one running point to another and talked with him during his run and at the various cadre rest areas.

"We don't have too many moments like this, and his smile and spirit people will always remember," a woman torch watcher said.

Charles L. Brown, chairman of the board of AT&T, wrote a letter to the 11,000 people "who performed so heroically for these Olympics, the gold medalists have nothing on you."

The letter was published in major newspapers throughout the United States next to a full page picture of one of the runners who exemplified the entire herculean effort of the people at AT&T, Phil Torres. The picture shows Phil carrying the torch high, with assuredness and pride.

Phil, a staff clerk in the legal department of Pacific Bell, was a coordinator for selecting the cadre teams. Like other cadre runners he had to face the inevitable letdown and sadness when it was over. "How can you want to train again for anything if it is not as great as the torch? I will never train as hard again for any run as I did for the torch run."

But Phil did make plans to run again. His choice of places? Where else but in Corvallis. "I write to a lot of people up there. We send pictures back and forth and they have invited me to come back. I am going back for a local marathon but I would go back even if it wasn't to run."

A runner who went out in the flame of glory as a cadre runner was AT&T system analyst Jerry Daniels.

Jerry Daniels was taken by his wife Rexanne in February of 1984 to the local emergency hospital after he had stopped running, complaining about severe back pains. The examining doctor told him that he had a seriously herniated disc, and recommended that he be operated on as soon as possible.

"How long after the operation will I be able to run again?" Jerry asked.

"About six months."

"I've got to run sooner than that. I'm going to be in the Olympic torch run."

"You can be in it but you won't be running."

Jerry and Rexanne went to another doctor who gave them the same prognosis. Another physician did the same. However eventually they were fortunate to have been introduced to a doctor who had what Jerry called a "more positive attitude" for getting him back to running.

That doctor estimated that in less than a month after the operation he could resume his training which up to that time had been 75 miles a week over various terrains. But Jerry was cautioned. "Don't become too aggressive with yourself. Trying to run too soon after surgery could very easily cause a reherniation of your disc that would pinch the nerve again and bring back your pain. Remember, the recently operated disc cannot stand up to the repeated pounding that running causes on the spine."

Rexanne and Jerry listened; the operation was a success and Jerry gradually began his training process a few weeks after the surgery. "I had gone into the operation barely able to walk and there I was a month later able to run again. It was an absolute miracle."

He trained well enough to be ready to participate in the cadre teams and ran for a week in Idaho, Washington and Oregon. Jerry then returned to his home and ran a few weeks later when the torch was in the Costa Mesa area.

"I ran 25 miles down there and had to quit. The pain had become so intense that I knew it was over. I wasn't a runner anymore. One of the doctors had said that swimming or cycling would keep me healthy. And they were right, but I was going to run with that torch. How else was I going to have the thrill of running along long stretches in the middle of nowhere and experience 500 people all of a sudden popping up as if from out of the ground to cheer us on? How many people get a chance to carry the torch through such towns as Fife and Windblock, Washington? I accomplished all I wanted to as a runner, and I would have been a long way from that goal if I hadn't run in the torch relay. It was something I had to do.

## THE TORCH AS A PARTY MAKER

It was a good reason to have a party. A great reason for a dance, a dinner and other grand waiting celebrations. The torch relay in fact became a giant party, a continuous infectious explosion of joy.

And it was not enough to have a stereo play the theme song from Chariots of Fire as you carried the torch by your home or business, nor was it enough to serve hors d'oeuvres to friends and business associates. Not for Bob Van Freda who held the complete on-the-job torch party.

Bob ran with the torch on a kilometer strip in front of his office on Olympic Boulevard in Los Angeles. The street was named for the 1932 Olympic Games held in the city. A four-piece band played and Bob served lunches to more than sixty people. He even made his own film which included a comedic rendition of him training for the run and scenes from his historic torch kilometer.

The movie showed AT&T Pioneers telling him he could not wear the wreath of leaves he had around his head (for fear of igniting during the run), and him autographing some of his more than one hundred requests for signatures. "I liked the attention but I don't think I'd like it all the time. But I would like to run with the torch every day. When I handed the torch off I thought about keeping it and running straight to the Coliseum (Bob ran a week before the torch entered the Coliseum).

"As it turned out, on the day the torch would enter the stadium I got up early and went to the starting point and ran for a few miles in front of the runners just to live out some of the excitement I still had left. There I was waving two American flags telling everyone the torch is coming."

The torch took its toll on Bob, however. He had planned to take a vacation during the Olympics by attending several events and be back to work after Closing Ceremonies. "It was about a month after the Games that I came down from the cloud that had risen when the Olympics came. And, it was not so much the Olympics but the torch that is to blame, if you can call it blame.

"But the memories keep going. People have sent me pictures. People I don't even know. One lady sent me a lot of them and said I was the only person in the Olympics who she knew personally. Whenever I leave my office I can't help but be reminded of it. Across the street is a printing business with a picture of me running with the torch in the window. The picture is signed, of course."

Having run in the relay has added a new dimension to Bob's competitive running. "Every time I run a marathon I think about carrying the torch. I get stronger and prouder of what I did when I think about it and all of a sudden I have a little extra energy. I get faster, and I want to run farther, too. Any time I ever think about stopping the thought of the torch comes through and I keep on going. It's amazing."

The film will always be there. Some people have suggested that he put it on a video screen in his office window and show it continuously so those passing by can see history being made over and over again. He had the film duplicated so he does not have to insure an only copy. "You couldn't put a price on what an only copy would be worth. And there is no price tag; there can't be on what the torch relay has meant to me."

Millions of people got a chance to meet one another during the torch relay. It was a great reason to meet someone you did not even know who was living or working right around the corner, even right next door.

In a small city bordering on the Pacific Ocean a high school principal and a gold medalist met, the outcome of which has been to the advantage of the kids of the school and the community.

Bob Eller, principal of Dana Hills High School in Dana Point, California, received a phone call from a parent of a student on the school's pep squad. The parent said he was a friend of an Olympic gold medalist and, "We should contact him to get him out for the torch."

The principal called him and the local banker whose institution was closely involved with events of the school to ask what could be done to celebrate the relay together. The banker called some of the local townspeople, balloons and food and drink were ordered, and the bank became a center point for the town.

Players on the football team dressed in their uniforms, cheerleaders and pep squad members clad in their jumping clothes, came by as did the Olympic champion and his Olympic champion wife.

"We all became instantly close. Everybody just automatically loved each other. It was just an automatic outpouring of good feelings," said one of the people in the crowd.

Close enough to where the Olympic athlete has since gone to the school to speak to groups of students. Close enough to where he has offered to help with the athletic program at the school, and close enough to where he has opened a bank account at the bank.

The Olympic champions were Bill Toomey, gold medal winner of the decathlon at the 1968 Mexico City Games, and his wife Mary Rand Toomey, gold and bronze medalist at the 1964 Tokyo Olympic Games.

Toomey was inspired by it all. "Wouldn't it be great if we could do this more often. Everyone has come together for this moment, and no one wants it to stop. We've all got a beautiful sense of being one."

## OLYMPIC EMPLOYEES CARRY THE FLAME

The Los Angeles Olympic Organizing Committee held several informational and staff morale meetings. One took place in March 1984, when 1500 employees were bused to Loyola Marymount University. After watching an Olympic film, a fashion show of Olympic athletic attire and a handball demonstration, Peter Ueberroth announced he was going to give away a kilometer to an employee. Instead of picking names out of a hat, he asked everyone to stand and through a process of elimination played a game which randomly matched employees with last names beginning with the letters M-Z, who had joined the Committee in '80, '82 or '84, and the last category was birthdates. When the countdown ended, two people remained standing, Nancy Strauss and Sarina Rosenkjar.

Nancy and Sarina ran on each side of a tunnel on Sepulveda Boulevard in the San Fernando Valley. Sarina ran the last kilometer on the west side of town, and Nancy ran the first kilometer on the Valley side. An AT&T cadre runner carried it through the tunnel.

Nancy basked in the glory of running with the torch as the highlight of her time working for the Organizing Committee. "Why not? I was a star for an hour. Mothers wanted their babies to have their picture taken with me. For a few moments I was right at the center of Olympic excitement. I was carrying the Olympic torch. The flame had come from Greece, was carried across the country by torch runners and would be lit in the Coliseum to begin the Games. I have never felt more American in my life."

On Wednesdays during lunchtime at the Committee's cafeteria, employees viewed footage of runners as they carried the torch through various parts of the United States. "As I watched and saw the emotion and excitement in each runner's face, my excitement and anticipation grew. About a week before running I was nervous. But that feeling quickly vanished during the bus ride that carried the torch runners to our starting points. As we drove through crowded streets, people were cheering, waving American flags and shaking our hands through the bus window. I lost the nervousness and had an incredible surge of energy. It was great. I loved it.

"Carrying the Olympic torch was one of the most wonderful experiences of my life. My family and friends all came out to watch me. When I ran the sun had just set and the view was clear and beautiful. It was a perfect night, absolutely gorgeous. At a party afterwards everyone wanted to hold the torch and be a part of this preciously unique symbol of Olympic history.

"That incredible feeling I had, while carrying the torch, lasted for weeks after the run. I glowed, talking about it afterwards, reliving the experience. The special bond torch runners have will last a lifetime. Sometime in the future, hopefully, we'll have a torch runners' reunion. I believe the torch has a special place in the hearts of all who were associated with it. I'm very proud that I was a part of this special and historic event."

Sarina has spent many fulfilling hours since the Games talking to groups about the torch and her run. Like many other runners she has mounted the torch in her home with an inscription of the date and time she ran alongside. "It's not something you want to put in a box and store away. You want it around you, so you can show it to others. Seeing it reinforces the spirit of the Games and continues to symbolize to me that I participated in something very special and wonderful."

# FROM DISAPPOINTMENT TO ADVENTURE

Seventy-year-old Pat Tambolleo of Huntington Beach, California was scheduled to run approximately 750 miles away from her home. She had recently suffered a heart attack and Tom Celori, who had been assigned to run near her city, opted to change places with her.

The average reaction to a faraway place was at first upset, however, when the runners reached those places they were glad of the opportunity to discover them.

"Who wanted to get up early in the morning to run three hundred miles away? I didn't but after I got there and ran I couldn't believe that I was so against it. I am actually glad I ran in a remote place. It made it an adventure," said Diana Issacs.

Diana had heard about the relay for a long time before she signed up to run. "I didn't know where I was going to get the money until I went on a trip with some friends to Las Vegas. I started betting a few dollars and I couldn't lose. I was on a roll and when I reached $3,500 I stopped. I thought, 'What am I going to do with this? I didn't earn it.' The answer came almost immediately. 'I am going to buy a kilometer.' It was a fluke. What else could be more worthwhile. I was given this extra money by luck so why not spend it on something that was fun and would help someone else. I wanted to run it right by my house like everyone else did, but having to run somewhere else turned out to be a blessing in disguise. I loved it."

Those who were not as happy as they wanted to be with where they had to run, however, were in a better position than those who did not run and were sorry they had not.

Susan Brower is a long-distance runner who had followed the route of the torch each night by television coverage. "As it got closer to the west coast I started wishing I had done whatever I needed to do to raise the money. It was just like the Olympics. The more you heard about them, and the closer it got to being here, the more you wanted to go to every event." Cara Pfeffer of Los Angeles epitomized the millions who were sorry they did not run: "It was the greatest thing I never did."

Everyone who ran the torch did not always want the honor. They did not see it as something special, not until of course it was on its way.

Dr. Charles Aronberg told his wife Sandra and his daughter Cindi that he was going to raise money for them to run when the torch relay was first announced publicly. Sandra and Cindi were not interested. As Charles put it, "It was something they thought was silly, like who need-ed to run around with a flare wearing shorts and a running top."

Charles knew how great it would be. He had attended four Olympic Games and had served on the medical staff for the 1960 Winter Games in Squaw Valley, California.

Within a few months of the beginning of the relay there was gradual change. "The progression went from negative to neutral to passive, to slightly interested, to somewhat more than slightly interested to in-terested, to willing, to enthusiastic, to eager, to overly eager to zealous about it. In the end there was nothing else they wanted to do. And by the time the torch was getting to the Los Angeles area it was the most important thing in their lives.

"When they ran it was like running on air... it was like that for all of us."

The Aronbergs were a complete Olympic family as they served as medical volunteers for the 1984 Games.

## SHORT TOUCHES OF THE FLAME

Reverend Donn Moomaw

"I feel that a lot of people were waiting for something like this to express their patriotism. The torch resurrected it all and made them childlike in their enthusiastic fervor," said Reverend Donn Moomaw who carried the torch with an autistic adult, Bill Kimmel, in Century City, California.

"But how do you capture an emotion like that? How do you evaluate it? It gave us such a euphoric feeling. I would like to know how to package that solid good spirit of appreciation people had for their country and for themselves. How can we sustain that spirit?"

Reverend Moomaw gave the benediction at both inaugurations of President Reagan and served as Commissioner of Weightlifting for the 1984 Olympics.

"The applause we got was for the idea, the continuity of the people being united in one cause. For me it was a unique athletic thrill." Moomaw was an All-American football player at UCLA during the 1950s. "I would have been just as thrilled if I were only part of the crowd. We were all one in the torch."

Practice and Fears

"I wasn't concerned about carrying the torch because I had practiced with weights," said Joan Cohen of Los Angeles who ran north of Pepperdine University along the Pacific Ocean. "I was worried about my hair. I didn't want it to catch on fire."

Other runners practiced with brooms, hammers, toilet plungers, bowling pins, baseball bats and homemade torches. Fears ranged from falling to becoming overcome by the exhaust from the cars and trucks in front of them.

Camp Pendleton Marine Base

The turnout and excitement generated by the relay was likened by many to how the country has reacted when winning a national war.

At the Marine Corps base at Camp Pendleton, California the armed services shared with the civilian population in celebrating the power of the torch. It was a dazzling performance. The entire Headquarters Battalion of the First Marine Division, all one hundred, ran in perfect cadence behind Sergeant Major Domenick A. Irrera, who carried the torch. "The military base did themselves proud," Irrera said.

"The battalion was so thrilled I don't think their feet ever touched the deck. It was a high point of morale for us. It was the best kind of victory, one with no casualties, and no war. And, the victory was for everyone," the sergeant major said enthusiastically.

## Knotts Berry Farm

At the annual employee-night party held by Knotts Berry Farm, races were held to choose a man and woman who would run with the torch. The winning runners ran consecutively exchanging the flame at Independence Hall of the amusement park when the torch arrived.

## The Japanese Citzens League

The Ventura County Chapter of the Japanese Citizens League became involved in sponsoring a kilometer due to the encouraging of Yoshitaka Sakayito. When the chapter collected enough donations for the run, they had no difficulty in deciding who would carry the torch for them, the one who had done the most to inspire their participation. "Sak"—Yoshitaka Sakayito.

## John Carlos

John Carlos, bronze medalist in the 200-meter dash of the 1968 Mexico City Olympics ... "You were the heartbeat of the people. It was sheer glory. It was like a fire that spread, and snowballed. It lit up the country, so much so that all anyone was concerned about was that the torch was coming."

## Bruce Furniss

Bruce Furniss, two-time gold medalist in swimming in the 1976 Montreal Olympic Games... "The torch relay took sports out of the Olympics and put the people into the Games. We were getting our country ready to welcome the world and embrace the Olympics." (Bruce was involved with the PR firm of Burson-Marsteller who helped with the public relations for the torch. Bruce did not carry the torch.)

## John Naber

John Naber, four-time gold medalist and silver medalist in swimming in the 1976 Montreal Olympics, ran on the day of Opening Ceremonies... "When they took the flame from my torch it was like letting the air out of me, but I was fortunate to have been revived with excitement that afternoon when I took part in the flag ceremony during Opening Ceremonies."

## Mike Reagan, son of President Ronald Reagan

"It wasn't who was carrying the torch. It was the torch that people were looking at. That was the symbol. People were feeling good about seeing the torch and that made them feel part of it. The torch was making us feel good about ourselves. Whoever carried the torch became a celebrity for that fleeting moment because they were carrying the symbol of America.

"I didn't want to give it up. It was definitely the most significant event that sold the Olympic Games. I don't think the Olympics would have had the impact it had without the torch relay."

## Ralph Miller of Balboa Island

Ralph Miller of Balboa Island, California, seventy-three, has to do the same thing for everyone who comes over to his home. He takes them over to the mantel and picks up his torch to show them.

"They have to touch it. And they want to take a picture with it. Things haven't changed since the relay. People are awed by it."

His identity has not changed either because of his run. "I was a celebrity for running and now I am referred to as the 'jogger in the torch relay.' Any kind of meeting I go to where I am introduced someone invariably has to make a comment about the torch.

"The first time I was recognized was at church. The minister announced it. Then at the Kiwanis Club. I like it. I hope it doesn't stop."

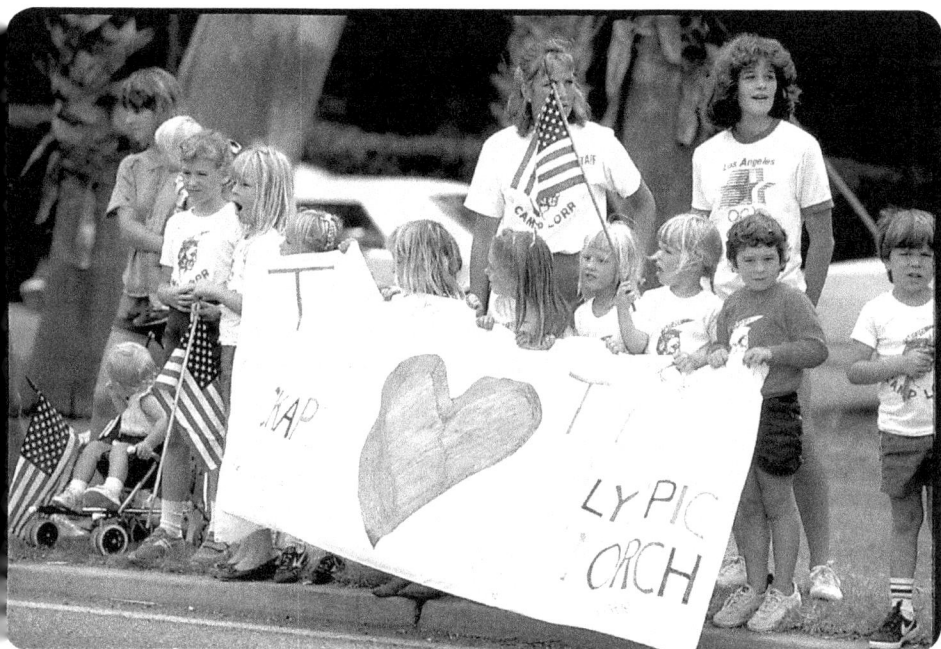
Children and parents awaiting the 1984 Olympic Torch.

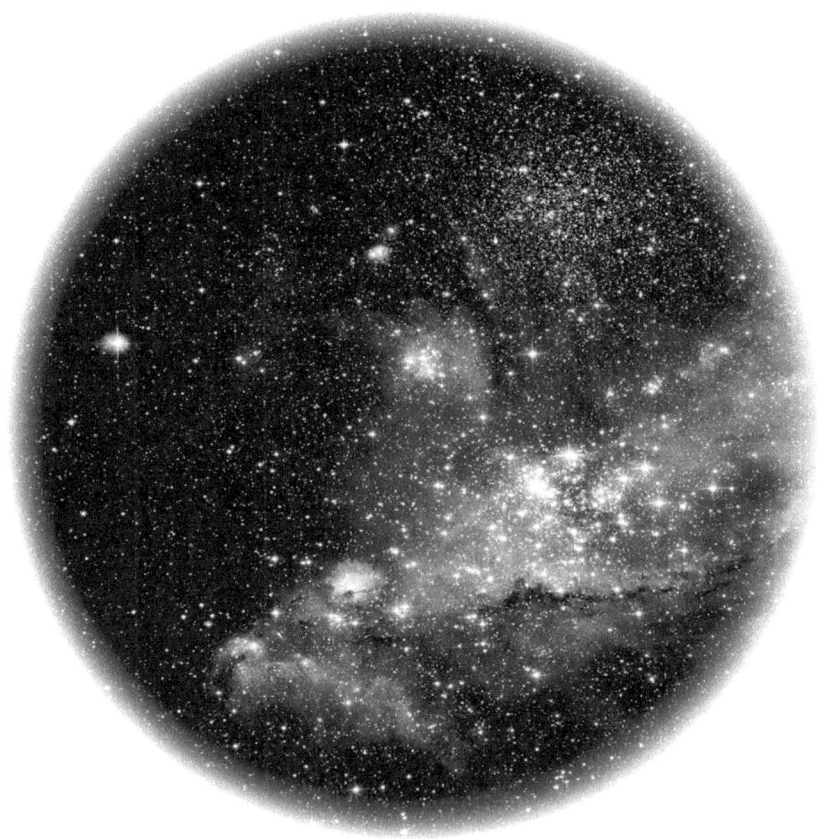

# Over the Wonder and Under the Why

*This is the first sports space story which questions the origins of the earth and the world through the metaphor of play. The girls, Katie and Kerri, wanted to have their own ideas for how the Earth and time began. They had read books and listened to people talk about it, and decided to create their own beliefs.*

"Why not?" Kerri said. "We need to think for ourselves."

"Of course, but I like what I have been taught," Katie said.

"You don't have to believe it, and it might not even be true, but at least we will have a version that we can say is ours," Kerri concluded. "Let me try. Well, in the beginning there was only space, quiet empty space, and two children appeared, as if it were the start of a magic show. The stars and planets also appeared right after, as if out of nowhere. And the more the children played, dancing among the stars and planets in space, the larger and wider and bigger the universe became, and whenever the children stopped play, the universe became smaller and smaller. It shrank. They played with one ball that was either a star or a planet, throwing it back and forth."

"Something that big?" Katie asked.

"The planet or star was small at the time they played," Kerri said. "They put it beneath their feet and began playing on it, and called it the Earth. And like everything else then, the more they played with it, the larger it became. The faster they played, the faster the Earth moved through space," she continued. "What do you think happened at the very beginning of everything?"

"The two children you mentioned were sitting on the rim of the universe, at the very end of it," Katie replied.

"How did they get there?" Kerri asked.

"They were just there, like magic, all of a sudden there they were," Katie continued. "And as a passing planet came by, they jumped on it and at that very moment the Earth began. You need at least a few kids and then you have an earth. And soon other planets appeared with other kids playing on them. And the more everyone played, the more the universe would exist. As long as no one stopped, the universe would go on and on and on," Katie reasoned.

"And what if they stop playing?" Kerri asked.

"They can't, for if they do, everything in space will soon disappear. It started with the magic of just being here, and it will stop when the kids don't want to play anymore or aren't allowed to," Katie explained. "Kids know this that is why they want to play all the time. They don't want to be the last person who stops playing, for then they will have to take all of the blame for the world stopping."

The girls sat and wondered about their theories, and then Katie said, "What about the center of the universe? Where do you think that is?"

Kerri replied, "That's simple. The center is the ball that is watched by the most people at any one time, and all of the explosions in space are caused by the change from one center of the universe to another."

"I believe that the ball I am playing with is the center of the universe," Katie said.

"I believe that at least one ball must be in motion on Earth to keep the Earth moving through space," Kerri said.

Katie said, "Will there ever be a time when the speed of everything that has ever moved in space equals the speed of all things that have ever played on Earth? I have often wondered who was the first person to ever run, to move quickly, and what was he or she given for the discovery?"

"Probably the gift of running forever. He or she just keeps on running," Kerri answered.

"And when will the distances of all the play on Earth equal the distances moved by every planet and star in space?" Katie asked.

They went down to the ocean and continued to talk. After watching children on swings on the sand, they wondered if their back-and-forth motion was what kept the water coming ashore and returning to the sea.

"Do the children running after the birds along the sand cause them to fly?" Katie asked. "My stillness sitting along the shore is balancing all of the motion of children at play everywhere."

Katie continued, "What new geometric forms can we create by connecting the lines of motion at play, and what motions of planets and stars moving through space are they like?"

"I can only imagine them," Kerri marveled.

As they looked into space, Katie questioned, "When will the numbers of friends made by play equal the number of elements that have collided in space? When will the time wondering about who is going to win games equal the time we have spent wondering about the mysteries of the universe?"

Kerri wondered, "If everyone jumps at once, will the Earth move within the rings of Saturn and will Saturn take the Earth's place in the universe?"

"Imagine millions of balls being shot into space all at once and millions of people being poured out of the sky onto Earth to begin play, or all balls being merged into one and moved into space to become another planet," Katie said.

"How much time do we have left in this world? What fraction of time have we finished? Are we halfway through or more, and how can we know?" Kerri asked.

"I can't imagine that we have ever cheered for our ideas as much as we have yelled and screamed for someone else's playing. Think about it. We have these ideas, and no one is cheering for them as much as even our cheering for others at play," Katie observed.

"Speaking of sounds, how many games where everyone screams and yells are equal to the sounds of the beginning of movement in the universe?" Kerri offered.

"How may screaming voices does it take to be heard by anyone listening on another planet?" Katie said.

The girls decided to go to the playground in their neighborhood.

On the basketball court, shooting alone, was a boy from their school. They were curious.

"We always see you shooting alone, and never in games with anyone else," Kerri said.

"If I played with others, I wouldn't be able to shoot as much as I want. I shoot to get a feeling of what it was like when the world began," Fred replied.

The girls smiled at each other.

"What do you mean, at the beginning?" Kerri asked.

"Well, the Gods of Play started everything by throwing planets and stars and moons into space, like I am throwing this ball through the iron-rimmed circle standing 10 feet up in the air," Fred explained. "The more I shoot, the more I believe that I am at the beginning of time and people and space, the magic making of everything."

"What about the balls that do not go through the rim and the net?" Kerri questioned.

"Those are the stars and planets that burned out, just disappeared," he answered. "I would like to believe that the world almost started a few times, and did not. I experience that when I miss a lot of shots."

"You really believe that?" Katie said. "Because we were guessing as to how the world began, and we too believe that it had to do with the play in the universe. Well, you know why you can't make every shot; you have to account for the missing stars."

"I have no proof that I can give anyone, this is just my belief. If enough people come to believe it, then we will be right," he concluded.

They all laughed.

"You don't have to prove it to anyone," Katie enthused. "As long as you believe it, it must be true."

"It is part of the fun of playing, creating your own version. Also, if I played with others, I would have to be better or worse than them, and I want to get better at shooting. I do not need anyone else to compare myself to," he said.

"We want to be playing whenever it is time for this world to end," Kerri said.

"Why?" Fred asked as he went to retrieve a ball that had missed the basket.

"We think that what you are doing when the end comes is what you will be able to do in the next universe forever," Katie said.

"The world will end when a ball that is hit or kicked or thrown into space keeps going and going, way beyond anyone's imagination.

And when it never comes back, get ready. It will have defied gravity, and we will be moving into another world," Fred surmised.

"What if you don't want to go?" Katie said.

"You won't have a choice. You know where I will be? Chasing a ball that did not go through the net, or watching another one go in," he said.

"We will be out here, hopefully, creating another story for how the next world begins," Kerri said.

"Hopefully, you always want to play. If you lose that need, the end will be near," he said.

The girls laughed together, as they chased one of Fred's missed shots off the court.

"Maybe we are playing in a world without boundaries, one that never began and cannot end. It was always here and it will always be here." He yelled to them as they ran through the grass chasing the ball as it bounced and rolled down the hill next to the court. The faster they ran, the faster and farther away the ball seemed to go.

# Credits

Pictures courtesy of:
    LPI/LA 84 Foundation
    LA 84 Foundation
    Richard Mackson, photographer
    Don Chadez, photographer
    Paul Slaughter, photographer
    NASA, ESA, A. Nota (ESA/STScI) et al.

    Stanley Silver, artist

    Football Illustrated 1936 cover

Books:
    *Don't Hit Him, He's Dead* by John McDonough and
    Paul T. Owens
    *Who's Kicking Now* by Ben Agajanian and Paul T. Owens
    *The Kicking Game* by Ben Agajanian with Paul T. Owens and
    Tom Landry

www.ingramcontent.com/pod-product-compliance
Lightning Source LLC
LaVergne TN
LVHW051516080426
835509LV00017B/2076